BIBLE MOMS

BIBLE MOMS

Life Lessons from Mothers in the Bible

AMBER ALBEE SWENSON

WESTBOW
PRESS

A DIVISION OF THOMAS NELSON

WestBow Press books may be ordered through booksellers or by contacting:

WestBow Press
A Division of Thomas Nelson
1663 Liberty Drive
Bloomington, IN 47403
www.westbowpress.com
1-(866) 928-1240

Because of the dynamic nature of the Internet, any web addresses or links contained in this book may have changed since publication and may no longer be valid. The views expressed in this work are solely those of the author and do not necessarily reflect the views of the publisher, and the publisher hereby disclaims any responsibility for them.

Any people depicted in stock imagery provided by Thinkstock are models, and such images are being used for illustrative purposes only.

Certain stock imagery © Thinkstock.

NIV – New International Version
Scripture taken from the Holy Bible, New International Version®. Copyright © 1973, 1978, 1984 Biblica. Used by permission of Zondervan. All rights reserved.

ISBN: 978-1-4497-8000-5 (sc)

Library of Congress Control Number: 2012923917

Printed in the United States of America

WestBow Press rev. date: 1/29/2013

For Sage, Simon, Audra and Addy—

May you guard ad keep His precious Word
to give to the next generation.

Contents

Lesson One Eve

Lesson Two: Sarah

Lesson Three: Rebekah

Lesson Four: Rachel and Leah

Lesson Five: Jochebed

Lesson Six: Manoah's Wife

Lesson Seven: Hannah

Lesson Eight: Rizpah

Lesson Nine: The Sidonian Widow and the Shunammite Woman

LESSON TEN: ELIZABETH

LESSON 11: MARY

LESSON 12: SALOME

Acknowledgements

Thank you, Lord. My words don't begin to describe your goodness and faithfulness.

Thanks, Steve, for giving me the freedom to do this, and Mom, for listening and praying and investing in me all these years.

Thank you to the Adult Spiritual Growth Team 2004(Tom Winter, Pastor Kom, Chris Thompson), who encouraged me from the beginning. Thanks also to Pastor Kom, who wouldn't listen to my excuses of being like Moses, and told me I was the one to teach this. I felt your prayers.

"In all my prayers for all of you, I always pray with joy because of your partnership in the gospel from the first day until now, being confident of this, that he who began a good work in you will carry it on to completion until the day of Christ Jesus" (Philippians 1:4–6).

Tips for Leading a Small Group Study

Congratulations! If God has led you to lead a group of women through this material, you are sure to have some interesting discussions, some disagreements, and most importantly, you will find the joy of Christian fellowship as you bond in the process of studying the Word together. I was pushed, shoved, and all but bound and gagged into leading the women in my church through these studies. I was happy to write them, but I certainly didn't want to get in front of people and read. I like to talk, but I hadn't been trained as a teacher. Here are a few things that helped me get through the first lesson and the years after:

Prayer: I asked a lot of people to pray for me. I asked them to ask for courage, and for the Lord's guidance and direction. Start each lesson with a prayer, too, for the Holy Spirit to come to you and to lead you to the truth.

Humility: Humility is helpful if you are able to admit the things you are struggling with in your life. I found that when I opened up, the other women opened up, too, and that's how we got to know each other, and how we knew how to pray for each other.

Time Management: It takes approximately two hours to go through each lesson. However, the best classes were the ones when we all shared our insight into how the scriptures changed our lives or the struggles we had. The most helpful insights often come from diversion. Try to limit the diversion, though especially if it goes down an avenue that doesn't bring insight to the group. If one person gets going on things specific to her that doesn't add to the group, try to encourage her and move on, then approach her after the study to talk more with her individually.

Be hospitable: Let each woman know she is important: Greet each woman when she comes. Introduce visitors to the group. Never put anyone down when they say something, even if they are way off. If you put them down, they may never come back and they might not learn the truth. To respond, try saying, "Does anyone else have a different take on this?" or, "I was thinking it meant this. What do you guys think?" Be gentle and considerate, and when you are totally at a loss for words, say a quick prayer for help.

Be prepared: You will need Bibles, and at times a dictionary. Work through each lesson beforehand so you are prepared with an answer if the group gets stuck.

Ask for volunteers: I don't make people read if they don't want to, or put people on the spot for answers. It helps if you go around the room and have each person look up a different passage to save time.

Holy Father, reveal Yourself to all those who work through this book. Enter their hearts, and plant in them the seeds of life. In Jesus' name. Amen.

Lesson One Eve

Topics for Further Study: The Nature and Deceptions of Satan, Resisting Satan and His Schemes, and The Nature of God.

READ GENESIS 2:15–25 AND GENESIS 3.

Devotion: The first chapters in Genesis reveal God's plan when He created man. His intention was for us to live in peace without sin forever. Adam lived in a perfect world, but had a void that neither his work in the garden or the companionship with the animals could fill.

God saw Adam needed a companion and a helper. In his infinite wisdom, God created a woman, and Adam finally felt whole. Eve completed Adam and provided a means of having and taking care of a family. Imagine the peace Adam and Eve had in the garden. There were no arguments, no power struggles, and no complaints. Imagine, too, their relationship with God. Genesis 3:8 talks of "the Lord walking in the garden in the cool of the day." Adam and Eve had access to God face to face.

If you get a group of women together, it is easy to see their husbands share a lot of the same characteristics, as do the women. Women tend to be the household coordinators, the emotional backbones of their families, and the people in the family who pay attention to the details, like dentist appointments and haircuts, feeding the kids healthy meals on time, dressing them in things that match or look somewhat clean, brushing their teeth before bed, etc. A lot of men will entertain the kids, but have a harder time making sure anything above their basic needs are met. Not all women are great about healthy meals and getting the kids to bed on time, nor do all men fit into a generalization. In our sinful world, each of us struggles in every role of our lives at some time or another. It does seem, though, that in general, not without exception, women do a better job of caring for the needs of the children. This shouldn't come as a big surprise to us. God created Eve to have the babies and He gave her the insight and abilities that she needed to care for her children. Adam was not created with the same identity.

Satan noticed the perfect peace Adam and Eve lived in and went to work to destroy it. He didn't go to Adam directly, but worked to tempt Adam through Eve. Do you notice this happening in your life? Have you been the voice of discontent, tired of a house or car or anything else that was too old or too small? Have you pushed your husband to buy things you couldn't afford? Have you encouraged him to use the copy machine or computer at work for personal use, misusing company resources? Have you urged him to overindulge in food or alcohol because you wanted to and you didn't want to do it alone?

Whatever the situation, it is important to recognize the areas in our lives where we may be tempting our husbands to sin. If we don't, Satan will keep working on us to cause divisions in our marriages. The division occurs when the bills arrive and there isn't money to pay them, or when your husband gets into trouble at work for doing something other than work, or when neither of you feel like dealing with the children because you've overeaten or drank too much.

With the first sin, a tearing took place. God and man were separated, as God was perfect, and man was suddenly sinful. Everything God had given Adam and Eve was ruined. The fields that had produced perfect crops sprouted weeds. Adam and Eve's relationship was perverted, and their own bodies brought them shame. Eve's ability to have children was scorned, so one of God's greatest blessings could only be attained with pain and misery.

Each time we sin, that same tearing takes place. It happens in our hearts when we feel the overwhelming guilt sin lays on us. It happens in our relationships when our sinful and hateful words and actions leave us lonely and disconnected from our husbands and children.

The only place we find peace is in the promise God gave to Adam and Eve that was fulfilled in Jesus' death on the cross. Our peace comes when we repent of our sinfulness and rely on Christ to pick us up. Jesus said in John 16:33, "I have told you these things, so that in me, you may have peace. In this world you will have trouble. But take heart! I have overcome the world."

For women, we also receive peace when we accept the role we have been given. Married life will be a constant struggle if we keep a tally on household or child-rearing chores. Paul told the Philippians, "Do nothing out of selfish ambition or vain conceit, but in humility consider others better than yourselves. Each of you should look not only to your own interests, but also to the interests of others" (2:3, 4).

No doubt about it; looking out for the interests of our husbands and children means making sacrifices. The question is; what will we sacrifice? Will it be a promotion at work that keeps us away from our family more, or maybe the pay of a full-time job as we cut back hours to spend more time keeping up with the family? Will we sacrifice personal time or sleep? Or will we sacrifice time with the children, our spouses, healthy meals, or clean homes? Rarely will a man offer to cut time at work to help out around the house, but accepting our roles as mothers and helpers to our husbands may lead us to do that. It can be hard to relinquish time at work, but the time spent getting things done at home can erase the friction and make the rest of the week so much better. With meals made and in the fridge or freezer, the argument over whose turn it is to cook disappears. Rummaging through laundry baskets in the morning rush is no longer an issue when the laundry is folded and put away.

The problem arises when it's too late for that. There is little flexibility when the children are in school full-time and the choices we made when they were little have left us in debt and unable to work less. But we can still make our families a priority. Stay-at-home moms can lose sight of that, too, and we may be tempted to make our houses or exercise schedules a priority above our children.

The time we put into our families is an investment, something that at times requires more of us than at others, but which brings lasting and sometimes eternal returns (Yes, the foundation that we give our small child today may indeed impact his or her plight for eternity).

Hosea 8:7 says, "They sow the wind and reap the whirlwind." The same thought is echoed in Galatians 6:7, which says, "A man reaps what he sows." If we don't put time into disciplining our children, into listening to them and making them a priority, we can't expect them to be well behaved, to listen to us, or to make our priorities theirs. Even when we do these things, children don't always follow through with the results we were hoping for.

After the fall into sin, God warned Eve there would be problems with her role. God said, "Your desire will be for your husband and he will rule over you" (Genesis 3:16). So much for their peace. Isn't it true that we desire to have what our husband has? We desire to have a job, to make our own way, to have someone else take care of the kids for a while. With sin, the appeal of being a helper became a curse, a feeling of oppression and being "ruled over."

To combat that, Paul said, "Your attitude should be the same as that of Christ Jesus: Who, being in very nature God, did not consider equality with God something to be grasped, but made Himself nothing, taking the very nature of a servant, being made in human likeness" (Philippians 2:5–7).

If Jesus came to serve, how much more should we? We don't have to grasp to have equality with our husbands by making sure he does at least as much work around the house as we do or by working as many hours as he does. Following Jesus' example, we can take on the nature of a servant and make the dentist appointments without grumbling, organize meals, and make a cleaning schedule the whole family can adhere to. We can take the initiative to get things done around the house in order to help our husbands and children. But we can't do it all. No one can. We will have to make some choices about what really matters to us. If we are stressed out and unhappy because the load is too much for us, chances are we aren't being very good wives or mothers.

The peace that Adam and Eve had in the garden will be ours again in heaven. Until we get there, Satan will be working on us, just as he did Eve. Sometimes we will resist; other times we may falter. Our hope is in Christ and in his words: "In this world you will have trouble. But take heart! I have overcome the world!" (John 16:33) With His help and guidance, we will make the right choices for our family and find fulfillment in doing so. With His grace we'll be forgiven and comforted when we haven't done so well and with His strength we'll get back on the right track.

Devotion Question: Whether a stay-at-home mom or a mother with a full or part-time job, we need to examine our motives for the choices we're making. The devil often tempts us to want more money, more clothes, and more things. If that is the case, we will never be content. A new house immediately begins the process of deterioration, as do new cars and new clothes. Someone will always have more than we will. Being content to be with our children and husbands can be a difficult thing when adult stimulation and prestige hold such strong allure. With God's help, we can change the attitude of our hearts and make being at home with our families more of a joy instead of a burden. We stay-at-home moms need to be on guard against self-righteousness, and also about making our children, and not our home or anything else, our priority.

Write down the temptations in your life right now that impact your husband and children. As you work through this Bible study, look for practical ways to overcome these temptations.

Topics for Further Study:

1. **The Nature and Deceptions of Satan**

   According to each passage, who is Satan?

   Luke 10:18; Revelation 12:7–9

   John 8:44

   1 John 3:8

   Read Job 1:6, 7, and 2:1, 2.

   What had Satan been doing before coming into heaven?

   _____

Read 1 Peter 5:8.

Why does Satan roam the earth?

_____

Read each of these passages, and write down what Satan is doing in each one.

Zechariah 3:1

Mark 4:15

Luke 13:10–17

Luke 22:31, 32

2 Corinthians 4:4

Satan is revealed as accusing the saints, stealing the Word from those who have just heard it, keeping a woman bound in an illness, wanting to crush Peter, and blinding unbelievers so they can't see God or His Word for what it is.

According to these passages, what does Satan look like when he comes to us?

2 Thessalonians 2:9, 10

2 Corinthians 11:13–15

Satan doesn't come to us looking dark and deceptive. If a plate of fat looked like a plate of fat, no one would be overweight. That temptation comes to us as a delicious dessert or mouth-watering, but calorie-laden, casserole. The men and women who live apart from God's ways are often attractive, seductive, and powerful. That is the power of deception.

Find in each of these passages why Satan works so hard to deceive us.

Matthew 25:41, 46

Revelation 12:12

Revelation 20:10

The cliché "misery loves company" says it all. Satan knows his time to trick and deceive is short and he knows he'll be spending eternity in hell. He's going to bring as many people with him as possible.

2. **Resisting Satan and His Schemes**

Read Matthew 4:1–11.

What methods did Satan use to tempt Jesus?

_____

Doesn't Satan often do the same thing to you? He rarely comes to me when I'm well rested, everyone is healthy, and my marriage is at its best. Temptation so often arises when we are at our weakest.

In Mark 8:36, we read, "What good is it for a man to gain the whole world, yet forfeit his soul?" Here we see the devil is ready to make that exchange. Serve me, he says, and I will give you money, fame, jewels, anything you want. Think of things that keep you from serving God the way you want to serve Him. What are they? Could they be distractions sent from Satan? Don't fall into his traps!

What did Jesus use to resist Satan?

_____

In order for us to use the Word against Satan, we need to be reading it, and praying to understand it, so Satan can't turn it around for his own use. We also have to keep the Word readily accessible to look things up when Satan tries to use it for his own ways. If your Bible is under a stack of books, on a bookshelf, or in a box, move it! Mine is often next to the bed, on the kitchen table, or on the couch. Keep it close by to use throughout your day.

What happened to Jesus once he resisted temptation?

_____

Read Ephesians 4:25–27.

What things does Paul say give the devil a foothold in your life?

_____

Why is it important not to give Satan a foothold?

_____

Did you know cellulitus, a bacterial infection of the skin, often starts with a tiny scratch, bug bite, or even a little bump? Once it starts, the infection spreads rapidly, often leaving a good portion of a leg or arm red and swollen. Satan is like that infection. He is a liar and if he can get a little sin in our life, he will work to convince us it is just that: a little sin. He'll show you how good you are in other areas of your life; even show you people who do things much worse than you. The problem is that any sin left unchecked is likely to spread into other areas. If you routinely show disrespect to your husband, you've opened yourself up to start belittling him. Once you've belittled him in your mind, it will spill out of your mouth, not just at home, but in public. If you surround yourself with other women who disrespect their husbands, there's no end to the means you'll use to make sure your wants and needs are fulfilled, regardless of him. I've seen it happen to very unsuspecting women who don't even seem to realize their talk is brash and disrespectful and completely humiliating to their husbands.

Paul warns us about anger and falsehood. The devil is the father of lies, so when we aren't being honest, we're speaking his native language. If you are in a foreign country and you hear your mother tongue, you are instantly drawn to the person speaking your language. When we lie, tell half-truths, exaggerate, or diminish the truth, the devil hears his native tongue and looks on you as a friend.

Anger is an emotion that can affect our thoughts, words, and actions. Prolonged anger and unresolved issues especially often lead to hostile thoughts, words, and actions.

Read James 4:7–10 and 1 Peter 5:8, 9.

What can we do to avoid Satan and his temptations?

_____

From these passages, what hope does God give us in the midst of trials and temptations?

Luke 10:17

1 Corinthians 10:12, 13

2 Thessalonians 3:3

3. **The Nature of God**

Read these passages and write down what each says about who God is.

Deuteronomy 10:14–17

Isaiah 44:24

Daniel 4:2-3

Matthew 3:16, 17

Write down the characteristics each passage tells us about God.

Exodus 34:6, 7

Leviticus 19:2

Deuteronomy 32:4

Psalm 34:8

Psalm 121:5–8

Psalm 139:1–4

Isaiah 40:28

Malachi 3:6

Luke 18:27

Compare these characteristics of God to the nature of Satan. God is forgiving, loving, and protecting. Satan, on the other hand, is an accuser. God is able to do the impossible. Satan causes infirmities. God is gracious, just, wise, and good. Satan blinds people from the truth of God and steals the Word from their hearts so they can't use God as their refuge and protection. With Satan is devastation, envy, and lies, but living with God is to live with compassion, wisdom, and patience. Who do you want to follow and whom do you want your children to follow?

If we're not modeling the characteristics of God in our homes, we ultimately show disinterest in God. God is someone to meet with on occasion and then leave at church. When you see the attributes of God in comparison to the attributes of Satan, you're left with a choice. What do you want the environment of your home to look like? Seeking God in your home not only brings about a house in harmony with the attributes of God, it also puts your children in line to inherit their eternal home. If you raise responsible children who always do their chores, who save and earn lots of money, who become successful in every area of their lives but have no time for God, you are setting them up for an eternity with Satan and he is glad to have them. If we don't make God a priority in our house, why will He be a priority to our children?

Read Matthew 25:34; Mark 16:16 and Acts 16:31.

Why must we believe in God?

_____

Read 2 Chronicles 16:9.

The devil roams the earth looking for someone to devour and to torment. What does God do?

_____

Read Ephesians 6:10–18.

While on this earth, if you choose to follow God, you are choosing to live at war with Satan. Look at their kingdoms. Satan's will end and is built on lies and lusts. When you become a soldier of God, you battle for an eternal kingdom, a kingdom that is just and good and decent. God wins and takes you to the happily ever after. That is worth fighting for!

Prayer to close the lesson:

Everlasting Father, Creator, I bow before You, humbled by Your majesty and in awe of Your creation. Thank you for the role You have given me as a wife and mother. Help me to serve my husband and children as You intended. Create in me a humble heart, and fill my life with joy and blessing. Satan would take all I have, but I ask that You guard my heart and mind. Help me to resist Satan so that I may honor You. In Jesus' name I pray. Amen.

Lesson Two: Sarah

Topics for Further Study: Nothing Is Impossible with God, Faith, You Can't Lie to God, and Patience

READ GENESIS 16:1–6; 17:15–21; 18:1–2, 9–15; AND 21:1–7.

Devotion: When Sarah gave Hagar to Abraham to sleep with, she was doing the only logical thing from her perspective. God promised Abraham in Genesis 15:4 that a son from his own body would be his heir. Since Sarah was beyond the age of bearing children (Genesis 18:11), human reasoning led her to believe Abraham needed to find a woman who could bear a child. After all, the promise didn't specifically mention her, though she might have assumed it did, since they were joined in marriage, and God wouldn't have asked Abraham to go outside the marriage to have a child.

As far as we know, Abraham's faith had not wavered when God promised him time and again that his descendents would be as numerous as the stars in the sky or grains of sand on the earth.

Abraham faltered only when Sarah came up with a tangible plan to get the child they had believed would come for years.

Like Sarah, our advice and actions can often sway our husbands, either to remain in the Lord or drift from Him. This is an important responsibility that requires prayerful stewardship. Even with a Christian husband and father, which not every family has, much of the family's direction comes from the wife and mother. If we are in the Word of God and prayer, we can be confident in God's direction for us and our family. Left to our own ideas, we often weave ourselves into a mess, and one sin often gives way to another and we start blaming people the way Sarah blamed her husband once Hagar conceived. Thankfully, we have a God who is well versed in rescuing us from ourselves!

In Galatians 4, Paul called Isaac the child of promise and the son born by the power of the Spirit (Galatians 4:28, 29). Abraham's plight would be an example for the people of Israel as they waited for their Savior. Abraham received a promise and was made to wait until the time was right for Isaac to be born in a miraculous way, just as the people of Israel would have to wait for God's perfect time to fulfill the ultimate promise to redeem His people and save them from their sin. At the time they were living it, Abraham and Sarah had no idea that God was using them as an illustration, nor did they understand their child of promise, born by the power of the Spirit, was a messianic symbol. God ended the illustration on the mountain where Abraham was about to offer Isaac as a sacrifice to God, because Isaac was sinful and would never be the true sacrifice that Jesus would be.

Though he made Abraham wait, God renewed His promise to him time and again (Genesis 12:2, 13:16, 15:4, 17:5, 18:10, 18:18) that Abraham and Sarah might not lose faith, but have a hope to cling to. Similarly, prophets throughout the ages pointed ahead to Jesus' birth so that Israel would remember the promise and continue to watch and wait.

Most of us expect results quickly when we ask the Lord for something and if we don't see things changing, we often give up, become disheartened, or take matters into our own hands. Until that day at Abraham and Sarah's tent when the Lord said, "About this time next year" (Genesis 18:10), Abraham and Sarah weren't given a specific time frame. Ishmael was thirteen years old at this point, and Abraham was ninety-nine. Twenty-five years passed from the time the Lord first promised to make Abraham's descendents like the grains of sand and the point that Sarah laughed at the entrance to the tent. The Bible does not tell us if Sarah's laughing was done in frustration, doubt, or another sentiment. It is interesting that Abraham reacted the exact same way (Genesis 17:17). We do know the Lord had sealed Sarah into the covenant with Abraham by changing her name from Sarai to Sarah and promising a son out of her own body (Genesis 17:16) just that year.[1] If ever there was a time to keep faith, it was then with God's promise so fresh.

Regardless of Sarah's intention, she lied to the Lord about laughing. How many times don't we also give up on our children or our ability to parent them out of lack of trust in God's grace to pull us through, finally getting to a point of laughing or being cynical when someone gives us encouragement? Perhaps at some time when you've struggled to make your young ones mind, you've experienced a tenderhearted older woman stopping you after a church service, or a grocery store clerk, or a neighbor who says, "I remember those days and it will get better." How often do we respond with, "I sure hope so" or, "Not soon enough!"

Whether walking through the trials of sleepless nights, temper tantrums, potty training, or rebellion of school age children or teenagers, we so often lose sight of the big picture, and the fact that our time with our children is fleeting. If we kept this in the forefront of our minds, disciplining would not be so frustrating. It would be a joy, knowing we have a short time to train our young ones, and we're being presented with the opportunity to teach our children a better, more godly way. We'd worry and suffer from unhappiness and discontentment far less if we could only trust God's timing and omniscient ways and wait patiently for Him to give us all the blessings He has for us when we're ready to receive them.

Sarah's actions with Hagar tarnished fourteen years of three people's lives. Hagar wasn't happy because she had to live with Sarah mistreating her. Sarah was jealous and humiliated and miserable. Abraham had to live around both women, which no doubt took its toll. Eventually Hagar and Ishmael had to be sent away in order to have peace. Hagar and Ishmael were sent into the desert to die, but God provided for them. Sometimes we are the result of other people's messes and we are the ones cast out of people's lives. If that is the case, God will provide direction and protection for us as He did for Hagar and Ishmael.

Sometimes we are the ones whose sinfulness has brought people and situations into our lives that never should have been. It can be very difficult to release these people. In Galatians, Paul backs up Sarah's decision to send Hagar and Ishmael away. When the consequences of our decisions keep us from following the Lord, it is up to us to amend those things. It can be as simple as remedying the bedtime routine that is geared more toward our happiness and convenience than our children's spiritual wellbeing. Five or ten extra minutes provide enough time for devotion and prayer. It can be as difficult as pulling our children out of a daycare that promotes things we shouldn't be allowing, or keeping our children home from a neighborhood party where movies contrary to our beliefs are being shown.

God told Abraham to name his son Isaac, which means laughter. There were certainly times when Abraham and Sarah stumbled, but overall, they showed incredible faith during twenty-five years of promise. Sarah's laughing at the birth of Isaac was laughter of great joy. We, too, experience that joy, when we seek God's counsel and go where He shows us to go. He will bless us and provide us with the tools we need to survive, and more, to experience God's joy, a joy that is all we could want or need; a joy that is complete (John 15:11).

Devotion Question: Think of the ways you advise your children and husband. Are you seeking and offering wisdom from your friends, a TV or radio show, and your parents, or are you going to the Bible in search of godly wisdom? As you work through this Bible study, consider these key thoughts and try to incorporate them into the way you pray and advise your family.

Topics for Further Study:

1. Nothing Is Impossible with God

Read Matthew 19:26; Mark 10:27; Luke 1:37; and Luke 18:27.

What is the significance of this same message written in four different places in the gospels?

_____

Read Numbers 23:19; John 1:17; and John 14:6.

Given what we are told about God and Jesus in these passages, why is it important that Jesus is the one telling us "nothing is impossible with God?"

_____

Read Numbers 11:18-23, 31, 32; Job 42:1–3; Luke 8:22–25.

What do these accounts tell you about God's ability to do wonderful things, and our comprehension of that ability?

_____

_____

The Bible is full of miracles; barren women having children (Sarah, Manoah's wife, Hannah, Elizabeth), the sun standing still (Joshua 10:13), sick people being healed, etc. Don't read about these miracles, like Sarah having a baby when she was ninety years old, and dismiss it as happening back when miracles happened, or worse, diminish the miracle by thinking people lived longer back then and it was not that remarkable. The Bible tells us Sarah was beyond the age of bearing children, so it was as remarkable in Biblical times as it is today. Ninety years old in Sarah's day was old, too. We are told, "Abraham and Sarah were already old and well advanced in years, and Sarah was past the age of childbearing" (Genesis 18:11). Numbers 23:19 says that God does not change. Humans don't change, either. We face the same issues today that people dealt with from the beginning of time. It's only two chapters in the Bible after Adam and Eve fell into sin that the world was destroyed because of wickedness. The jealousy, backstabbing, gossip, and evil plotted against us today are exactly the same as in Noah's day. We have nothing in our lives that God isn't able to overcome. What seems so huge to us is completely possible for God to handle: addictions, out-of-control children, the weight we can't seem to lose, or trouble with your in-laws. With God's help, all things can be conquered.

2. Faith

Read Hebrews 11:1, 6, and 11–13.

The writer of Hebrews used the words "sure" and "certain" in his definition of faith. What significance does this have?

My dictionary[2] defines sure as "impossible to doubt." How would a word such as "hopeful" in place of sure change the context of this definition?

_____

What two things does Hebrews 11:6 tell us we must believe in order to be pleasing to God?

_____

_____

How do we go about earnestly seeking Him?

_____

Read Matthew 9:22; Mark 5:34; 10:52; Luke 7:50; 8:48; 17:19; 18:42.

What did Jesus say healed these people?

_____

Read Matthew 13:58; 17:19–21; and Mark 6:5,6. What wonderful miracles did these people experience?

_____

Notice the contrast between what those people who had faith received and what those without faith received. Jesus could have healed any of the people present. He chose not to heal because of their lack of faith.

Read Matthew 9:27–30.

What question did Jesus ask the men?

_____

Notice Jesus didn't heal the men immediately. The men followed him, and when Jesus went inside, they followed him in there. If God were to say to you concerning the seemingly impossible situations in your life, "According to your faith will it be done to you," would you see any results, or would you be like the people who went away without seeing anything?

Read Mark 9:21–24.

All of us experience moments of doubt. Here we see the proper way to respond: "Lord, I do believe; help me overcome my unbelief!" We've already established the fact that God can do the impossible. Sometimes He's just waiting for you to believe.

Read Joshua 10:5–14.

The army of Israel had marched all night long in order to take the Ammorites by surprise. It was midday when Joshua said, "O sun, stand still over Gibeon, O moon over the Valley of Aijalon" (10:12). The army of Israel fought for thirty or more hours straight, and this after an all night march! It wasn't the Israelite army that defeated the Ammorites. It was the Lord. The Lord threw the Ammorites into confusion (10:10) and hurled hailstones from the sky, killing more men than the warriors of Israel (10:11). Joshua and the army of Israel showed up and believed God's promise to deliver the Ammorites into their hands, and the Lord took care of the rest.

What difficult, seemingly impossible situation are you in right now? Is it a husband who is totally uninvolved with your family? A child who is afraid of the dark? An older child who is straying from the Lord? A financial burden that seems about to break you? An illness or family member's addiction? None of these things are too big for God, so give them to Him and trust His ability to work it out. Just be prepared, because often God's solution is much better than what we could come up with, as are the blessings that come after.

List the situations in your life that seem overwhelming right now, and use it as a prayer list in days and weeks to come.

3. You Can't Lie to God

Read 1 Samuel 16:7; Proverbs 21:2; and Isaiah 29:13.

What basic truths do these passages teach us?

_____

Why is it important to understand that we cannot lie to God, whether in our prayer lives, thought lives, or worship lives?

_____

Hebrews 11:6 tells us God rewards those who earnestly seek him. Earnestly means genuinely, truthfully, "… with serious intent."[3] If we are seeking the Lord, but are only saying what we think He wants to hear, we are not putting ourselves in a position to be rewarded by Him, because He looks at our hearts and our intentions.

Read these passages and write down which emotion David is experiencing.

Psalm 51:1–7

Psalm 58:1–3, 6

Psalm 64:1

Psalm 69:1–3

Psalm 100

Instead of calling your mom or a friend, which could lead to gossiping, or enticing, or assumptions as to why a person did what they did, go to the Lord and let Him know the condition of your heart. He's the only one who can change the way you feel and the details of the situation. Besides, we have the assurance that He rewards those who earnestly seek Him. There is no clause that states He rewards the person who only comes to Him with praise, or who doesn't complain. He rewards earnestness.

4. Patience

Read 2 Peter 3:8, 9.

Peter tells us God is not slow in keeping his promises, but rather patient with us. What does this mean?

_____

Could it mean that sometimes God has blessings in mind for us, but He's waiting for our hearts to be in the right condition to receive them? I have a friend who tried for three agonizing years to conceive her second child. After the child was born, six years after her first, she contended God knew what He was doing spacing her children that way. Often it is the struggles in our lives that teach us patience, compassion, and endurance. I have learned that when you are in the midst of suffering, trying to wait patiently on the Lord, a word of encouragement can mean the difference between barely making it and enduring. When you think of patience, don't think only of your own struggles, but find someone you know who is going through a hard time and encourage them to trust in the Lord.

Read Psalm 37:5–9.

David gives us several commands for living. List them.

Commit

Trust

Be

Wait

Refrain

Turn

Do not

Hope

To be still before the Lord is to go before Him in submission, to ask His guidance, and to seek His way to resolve an issue, instead of offering your own ideas. It also means going into His presence and simply saying, "You know what's going on, Lord.

I'm not going to cry or whine about it this time. I'm just going to give it to You."

Just as it is nearly impossible to get someone else's point of view if we do all the talking, to get God's point of view, we sometimes need to just come into His presence and listen. For four days after my husband's father died unexpectedly, I was completely unable to pray, except to say to the Lord each night, "I'm here." I was hurt and tired and in shock and completely still before the Lord.

Wrath is violent anger. Think about how you deal with your children. When you lose your patience with them, do you turn to wrath or from wrath? Turning from wrath is keeping your cool, staying calm, and dealing with the situation without resorting to yelling or any form of punishment in anger. It is important to punish your children, but it is equally important to do it out of love instead of anger. How do you answer your husband when he asks you for his socks, or lunch, or whatever, when you're in the process of feeding the baby, finding your daughter's lost belt, and getting your sons shoes tied? Maybe you aren't in the middle of a struggle in your life right now that requires patience, but you could use a dose of patience in dealing with your children or your husband. Look at these seven steps as a practical guide to attaining the patience you desire.

Read Psalm 37:18-19, 23–26.

What rewards do we receive when we follow the commands listed earlier?

1. (37:18)

2. (37:19)

3. (37:23)

4. (37:24)

5. (37:25)

6. (37:26)

Sarah's life showed the disappointments that come with doing things our way. God's way offers so much more. Make the effort to seek God, be honest with Him, and wait for Him. The rewards outweigh the effort.

Prayer to close the lesson:

Heavenly Father, forgive me for the many times I have taken matters into my own hands and made a mess of my life. Teach me to seek You, so it is You guiding me through this journey and directing my steps. Take my hurts, problems, worries, and fears and turn them into something beautiful to be used for Your glory. In the stillness of my time with You, speak to my heart, and fill my soul with peace. In Jesus' name I pray. Amen.

LESSON THREE: REBEKAH

Topics for Further Study: Favoritism,
Mothers-in-law and daughters-
in-law, and Forgiveness.

READ GENESIS 24:34–66; 25:19–28; 26:34-35; 27:1–17, 41; 28:1.

Devotion: Rebekah was the one chosen by God to be Isaac's wife, and to carry on the line of the Savior and the blessing of descendents as numerous as the stars and grains of sand. The Lord, who looks at the heart (1 Samuel 16:7), handpicked Rebekah, to, among other things, comfort Isaac in the loss of his mother.

It is a comforting thing when we see the hand of the Lord working things out in our lives and putting pieces together. Both Abraham and his servant put their trust in God and He did not disappoint them. Often we are reluctant to give the Lord full control of a situation until it is not going well.

Laban and Bethuel's reaction is equally commendable. They acknowledged God's hand in the situation, even trusting their daughter and sister to go away with a total stranger. How many people would do that? Often when you share with people the way God is working things out for you, they become skeptical, even critical of what you know is the Lord working. I've had enough "coincidences" in my life to no longer believe in coincidence. I believe in the hand of God, just as Abraham, his servant, Laban, and Bethuel did.

Rebekah was Sarah's nephew's daughter, and she shared a great many traits with her great-aunt. Both were very beautiful. Sarah left her homeland with her husband, and Rebekah left her homeland to go to her husband. Both were barren, and both took matters into their own hands at some point; Sarah in giving her husband to Hagar to get a son, and Rebekah in tricking Isaac into getting Esau's blessing.

God told Rebekah her older son would serve the younger, so why was it Isaac said, "Be lord over your brothers, and may the sons of your mother bow down to you" (Genesis 27:29) to the man he thought was Esau? Could it be Esau, who sold his birthright for a bowl of stew, got his zealousness for food from his dad, Isaac, who, Genesis 25:28 says, also had a taste for wild game?

Rebekah did accomplish God's will, but she stepped on Isaac and Esau to have it that way. Would a different way, such as talking to Isaac after Esau left and reminding him of God's words to her, have worked? Or, did God work through Rebekah's deceit to accomplish His will, much the way He worked through Rahab's lie to save the spies, and Samson's engagement to a Philistine woman to bring revenge on the Philistine people? God had already determined the Savior would come from Jacob, and nothing Isaac said or did would change that.

If Esau got his ability to be swayed by a meal from Isaac, then Jacob got his partiality to deceit from Rebekah. What traits are your children inheriting from you? I think we'd all like to say, "My strong faith, gentleness, discipline, patience, and steadfastness to prayer." A more honest answer may include becoming easily angered, being impatient, cursing, lying when it is convenient, overeating, finding ways to get out of obligations, etc.

Jesus said, "Do not judge, and you will not be judged. Do not condemn and you will not be condemned. Forgive and you will be forgiven. Give, and it will be given to you" (Luke 6:37,38). To Jacob, He could have said, "Deceive and you will be deceived."

If we read further in the account of Jacob, we'd see Jacob deceived Isaac to get the blessing, and then he was deceived by Laban and tricked into marrying two women. He deceived Laban and took Leah and Rachel and all his children and left Laban while Laban was away shearing sheep (Genesis 31:21), then was deceived by Rachel, who stole Laban's household gods without Jacob knowing. Her deception could have cost Rachel her life. Because Jacob had no knowledge of her taking the gods, he swore, "[I]f you find anyone who has your gods, he shall not live" (Genesis 31:32).

Jacob took advantage of Esau's hunger and impulsiveness to get the birthright, and Laban took advantage of Jacob's love for Rachel and got free labor for fourteen years and changed his wages ten times over the remaining six years Jacob worked for him (Genesis 31:41).

Sounds like a vicious cycle, doesn't it? Have you ever noticed the same thing happening in your life? I once heard a politician say in a debate, "Insanity is doing the same thing over and over and expecting a different result."[4]

When we pray and give our problems to the Lord, we can expect Him to work them out in His time and in His way. When we manipulate situations to get things done quicker or our way, chances are there will be consequences. When we turn to a bottle of wine or beer, a bowl of ice cream, a cigarette, or a shopping spree to make us feel better, we are always left with emptiness: an empty bottle, an empty bowl, an empty hand, or an empty wallet.

Fullness can only be found in Christ. Jesus said, "I have come that they may have life, and have it to the full" (John 10:10), and Paul says, "You have been given fullness in Christ, who is the head over every power and authority" (Colossians 2:10).

What are some of the problems that occur in your house over and over? Children who disobey their parents bring more hardship than blessing to their parents. If you are going crazy due to your children's disobedience, take a closer look at the situation. Are you spending quality time with your children? Children can sense when they are a distraction instead of a priority, or when you are preoccupied with other things. How is your discipline? Are you consistent, or do you get lazy about it and only discipline one out of every five or six times your children need it? Do your children feel loved? Are you strict and on top of things with the discipline, but fail to show your children how much they mean to you? We all fail to do these things perfectly, but we can do them routinely. We can break the cycle so the same disobedience won't keep occurring.[5]

The most important thing we can do is pray for God to change our children's heart so their rebellion turns to obedience.

How is your marriage? If you are consistently arguing about the same things in your marriage, stop arguing, be quiet, and give it to the Lord. Peter said that, "the unfading beauty of a gentle and quiet spirit…is of great worth in God's sight" (1 Peter 3:4). Stop arguing and start praying for the Lord to bless your husband to make good choices and to do the right thing. You cannot change your husband, and often you can't change your circumstances, but God can change both. He can also change you if that's what needs changing.

Rebekah's deception caused her to miss out on years of Jacob's life. Because Jacob fled from Esau, he went to Laban as a homeless man and was subject to work for Laban instead of going to him and asking for a wife to return to his home the way Abraham's servant went and asked for Rebekah.

Rebekah is never mentioned after the blessing, which may mean she died before Jacob returned. Her favorite son was gone, Isaac was old, and Esau's wives caused a great deal of misery to her. How blessed is the family whose mother promotes peace between her children and lives in peace with her husband! The rewards of your hard work, whether it be putting forth the effort for discipline, or biting your tongue when angry words come so much easier, will bring years of joy to you. Lord, help us to do these things!

Devotion Question: What generational sins are you dealing with? What are you going to do to keep from passing these things on to your children?

Topics for Further Study:

1. **Favoritism**

   Read Leviticus 19:15, Romans 2:11.

   What do these passages tell us about the character of God?

   _____

   Read Ephesians 6:9.

   What makes us all equal before God?

   _____

   Read James 2:1–9.

   Who was causing the problems in the congregation James was talking to?

   _____

   _____

   What does that tell you about making judgments based on what you see?

   _____

   What does that tell you about your children?

   _____

Why ultimately must we not show favoritism, whether with our children or anyone else? (2:9)

_____

_____

Do you show partiality toward one of your children? What is it that makes you favor that child? What can you do to make sure your children all feel equally loved in your eyes?

_____

_____

2. Mothers-in-law and Daughters-in-law

Read Genesis 2:24.

Where is your allegiance to be once you are married?

_____

Read Mark 7:9–13.

One of my Bibles says, "Corban. The transliteration of a Hebrew word meaning 'offering'. By using this word in a religious vow, an irresponsible Jewish son could formally dedicate to God (i.e., to the temple) his earnings that otherwise would have gone for the support of his parents."[6]

Jesus made the point that it was pleasing to God for a grown man to help his parents, to honor them, and to not curse them. If we incite our husband against his mother aren't we causing him to not honor his mother and maybe even curse her?

_____

Read Ephesians 6:2, 3.

Of what benefit would it be to us to help our husbands honor their parents?

_____

_____

Read 1 Kings 2:19.

How did Solomon treat his mother?

_____

Read Proverbs 23:22; 1 Timothy 5:4[7]

How long are we to show honor to our mother or mother-in-law?

_____

What does Paul say is pleasing to God?

_____

Read Matthew 10:37 and Acts 5:29[8]

When would it be OK to not listen to our mother-in-law's advice, or take issue with something she asks of our husband?

_____

3. **Forgiveness**

Though we didn't read the entire account of Jacob and Esau, if we had, we would have read that when Jacob returned home after twenty years, Esau met Jacob joyfully, having forgiven him of all wrongs.

Read Colossians 3:12, 13.

Why does Paul tell us to forgive?

_____

Read Matthew 18:21, 22.

How often are we to forgive the people in our lives?

_____

What does that mean?

_____

So often I hear Christians talking about forgiving the people who have hurt them, but staying away from those people, or cutting them off so they don't get hurt again. Peter was being generous by some people's standards by offering forgiveness seven times. Many people say, "I'll forgive you this time, but if you ever do this again, you're on your own."

Jesus said forgive a person as often as they sin against you. Paul said, in Colossians 3:12 and 13, that we are to "clothe [ourselves] with compassion, kindness, and humility," and "bear with each other." When I think of the word clothe, I think of something I do each day. Paul didn't say if you aren't treated the way you deserve to be treated, leave and never come back. He said bear with each other. Jesus didn't say three strikes and you're out; he said forgive as often as you are sinned against.

Submission, forgiveness, and humility are not things that come easy, nor are you going to find a cheering section in the secular world telling you what you are doing is right. Paul said, "We are not trying to please men but God, who tests our hearts. We were not looking for praise from men, not from you or anyone else" (1 Thessalonians 2:4,6).

God tests your heart to see if you will be obedient to Him and call Him master, or if you'll look for approval from your friends or family or co-workers. I guarantee you will find people to agree with you when you hold a grudge and cut people off. When you do things God's way, you can expect persecution. Jesus said, "If the world hates you, keep in mind that it hated me first. If you belonged to the world, it would love you as its own. As it is, you do not belong to the world, but I have chosen you out of the world. That is why the world hates you. Remember the words I spoke to you: 'No servant is greater than his master.' If they persecuted me, they will persecute you also" (John 15:18–20).

Read Matthew 6:14; Matthew 18:21–35; and Mark 11:25.

Why must we forgive those who sin against us?

_____

In the parable of the unmerciful servant, what is God showing by the different amounts of money the men owe?

_____

How can you teach your children to forgive as God tells you to forgive?

_____

_____

Prayer to close the lesson:

Dear Father, teach me to acknowledge You in my life. Let me inquire of You before I do things so I am assured of Your blessing. I know You give great gifts, often far better than I could obtain or even desire. Give me the grace to be good and kind to my mother-in-law and all people. Bestow on me a rich supply of mercy to forgive others the way You forgive me. Without You, I will fail at both these things, but with You, I can form lasting and loving relationships. Because of Jesus' sacrifice I am able to come before You. Hear me, in His name. Amen.

Lesson Four: Rachel and Leah

Topics for Further Study: God Works Around Our Weaknesses, God's Time, Joy and Contentment, and Jealousy.

Read Genesis 29:16-30:24, and 35:16-20.

Devotion: In Genesis 28:14, God promised Jacob on his way to Laban's house that his "descendants would be like the dust of the earth." It seems when Laban tricked Jacob into having two wives it worked to fulfill that promise. The twelve sons of Jacob, who would later be known as the twelve tribes of Israel, became the foundation of Old Testament society. How could it be that God worked through a sin, and not just one, but several, to produce the cornerstone of Jewish society?

Leah did not have a lot going for her. The Bible tells us Rachel was a beautiful woman with a nice shape, but we are told nothing of Leah except that she had weak eyes. It makes you wonder what all was left out of that description. It alludes to the fact that Jacob was attracted to Rachel and fell in love with her, but Leah had nothing to attract Jacob to her.

Laban may or may not have realized that just getting Leah married didn't mean she would be loved. Leah's life offers assurance that God loves us even when a man or any other human; a mother, sister, father, brother, or friend, doesn't. Genesis 29:31 says, "When the Lord saw that Leah was not loved, he opened her womb, but Rachel was barren." As in the study of Sarah, we see God measuring His blessing. Sarah was beautiful and wealthy and the wife of a powerful man, yet she was barren. God blessed Rachel with looks and the love of her husband, but he made her wait to have children.

From this passage, we can be assured that all children come about because of God's grace. He opens the womb of those He allows to bear children, and closes others. Sometimes His grace is sufficient for the time being. Jacob understood this when he became angry with Rachel for demanding a child and said, "'Am I in the place of God, who has kept you from having children?'"(Genesis 30:2). The Bible assures us that with children, as with all other aspects of our lives, God is in control.

With each son, Leah hoped to gain Jacob's love. Even after her sixth son, Leah tried to gain honor and favor from her husband. The struggle each woman had to have more children alluded to the fact that there was jealousy in the two sisters' lives. Leah's accusations in Genesis 30:15 that Rachel took her husband were not accurate; after all, Rachel had been promised to Jacob long before Leah was given to him. The jealousy of Rachel and Leah; Rachel over Leah's children, and Leah over Jacob's love, allowed the women to do unbelievable things, the epitome of which was giving their husband another woman to sleep with to bear children. It was only two generations back when Sarah tried the same thing, only to cause herself to suffer more.

Deuteronomy 29:29 says, "The secret things belong to the Lord our God, but the things revealed belong to us and to our children forever, that we may follow all the words of this law." What has God revealed to us from Rachel and Leah's life?

First, we see God works around our weaknesses and our sins. The Savior would come from Judah, a son of Leah, but Rachel's son Joseph saved Judah and all of Jacob's family from starvation. Despite Laban's deception, God blessed the offspring of both of Jacob's wives. It's important to note that Judah and Joseph were Leah and Rachel's sons, not the sons of their maidservants. Jacob had been tricked into marrying the two women, but it was his decision to go along with the games his wives played for more children. He had children with other women, but God's blessing was not on them in the same way as his wives' children. It is also worth noting that God chose the line of the Savior, not Jacob, who would have had Rachel be his only wife.

Second, we see from Genesis 30:17 and 22 that both Rachel and Leah called out to God in their pain and He listened to them and remembered them, not in their time, but His. Despite the fact that Rachel had so much, God didn't keep her from having children altogether, He just allowed Leah to have them first.

Third, children in and of themselves cannot bring about happiness or a fulfilling marriage. Leah bore seven children, but

Jacob always loved Rachel. Only God can bring about happiness and fulfillment in all aspects of our lives. Leah, it seems, finally recognized that. Even with her third son she was hoping to win Jacob's love, but by her fourth, she just praised the Lord for what she had. It is an awesome example for us to love our husbands for what they are. If you look for your husband to fulfill all your needs and be everything on your wish list, you are sure to be disappointed. But, if you look to the Lord for everything you need and thank Him for what He's given you, instead of concentrating on what you or your husband lack, you are bound to feel contentment instead of disappointment. Had Rachel come to that realization, she would have saved herself years of misery.

Finally, the sin of jealousy, like any unchecked sin, ruins a relationship. Leah and Rachel spent their lives in competition. It would be very difficult to share your sister's husband for sure, and in fact, it should never have happened. We see with Jacob's story a full illustration of the domino effect sin has; the sin of deception led to polygamy, to the sin of jealousy, to bickering, to using children, and to the act of childbearing as a means of pride. Rachel and Leah's plight illustrates the time and energy wasted on ill feelings. In fact, that determination to have another child cost Rachel her life. Wouldn't it have been wonderful if Leah had seen the Lord was blessing her with children and she had shared her children with Rachel? What if Rachel had seen Leah's four children and, with prayer, gotten through the jealousy and helped Leah raise her children until the Lord gave her one of her own? Years wasted with ill feelings cannot be replaced.

It is also good for us to take note of the fact that it is easy to excuse sin and make false assumptions about God. In Genesis 30:17, Leah became pregnant with her fifth son, a son she asked for. We are told, "God listened to Leah and she bore Jacob a fifth son." The next verse says, "Then Leah said, 'God has rewarded me for giving my maidservant to my husband'" (Genesis 30:18). God doesn't reward sin. Verse 17 assures us with, "God listened to Leah" that her fifth son, like all children, was a gift of grace.

It would be easy for us to shake our heads and say this is one screwed up family, but if we are honest about it, all families are sinful and have their shortcomings. Walking with the Lord and staying in the Word can diffuse and reduce the impact of our sinfulness. As we study the Word, we learn to love and forgive as Christ forgave us, and that is the balm that heals family wounds.

Devotion Question: Lamentations 3:40 says, "Let us examine our ways and test them, and let us return to the Lord," and Romans 12:18 says, "If it is possible, as far as it depends on you, live at peace with everyone."

Take some time today and examine your life for the sins that cause you pain. What issues come up in your marriage over and over? What family issues do you have in your power to make better? Is there a friend you have become estranged from, or a person at church you don't talk to anymore? Be the one to take the first step. Think about these things and pray about these things. Do what you can to make the proper adjustments before too much time goes by.

Topics for Further Study:

1. God Works Around Our Weaknesses

Read Romans 15:1–4.

With the account of Rachel and Leah, it is easy to get disheartened by the mess of their situation. God assures us in this passage that the elements of sin and the problems caused by it were included in the Bible for two reasons. What were they?

_____

What encouragement can we find from the deceit, jealousy, pain, and misery of Rachel and Leah?

_____

What does this passage say about those people in our life who continually fall into sin? (15:1)

_____

Why do we need to bear with those who are weak? (15:2)

_____

Read 1 Corinthians 1:26–31 and 2 Corinthians 12:7–10. Paul suggests God actually chooses to work through the weak person; the man or woman with little influence or wisdom. When we are small, God can fill us up with Him. Just as in the lesson on Sarah, when we read of the Israelite army's defeat of the Ammorite kings, and the victory which was secured by God's hand, we can be assured when

God works through us, it is Him, not us, achieving the successes for His kingdom. Paul said his weakness was actually given to him to keep him humble so God could continue to work through him. If and when we get too big to effectively work in God's kingdom, God will find ways to keep us humble and weak so that we are useful to Him.

Have you ever worked with anyone who thought they were too good for the job they were doing? Did you notice what kind of job they did? People who are doing something they feel is beneath them typically do poor work and complain a lot while doing it. Rarely do they last long. Whether teaching Sunday school or taking out the trash at church, we would do well to do whatever needs to be done, willingly. Humility brings about good service and produces results. Look at the effect of Jesus washing the disciples' feet. He did the most menial of tasks so they would, in turn, serve one another without bickering after He was gone.

What weaknesses do you struggle with? Do you think they draw you closer to the Lord?

_____

Read Exodus 4:1–14 and Jeremiah 1:6–8 and 17.

Moses and Jeremiah used their weaknesses as an excuse not to serve in God's kingdom. Did God accept their excuses?

_____

Are you using a weakness as an excuse not to serve at church or in your community? How do you think God would respond to that?

_____

Read Romans 12:3–8 and Philippians 4:13.

List the gifts in verses 7 and 8.

_____

_____

Which of those are you good at?

_____

_____

Which one represents your greatest weakness?

Has God called you to do any of these things? Have you been asked to serve in any capacity at your church? Have you been asked to teach a Bible class or Sunday school class? Have you been asked to consider a leadership role, or to give more money to a building or general fund? Which of these things did you list as something you are good at? God will use you, if you are willing. Consider how you can serve God according to the abilities he has given you.

2. God's Time

Read Daniel 12:7–13 and 2 Peter 3:8,9.

What has God revealed to us about time, namely his sense of time?

What implications does that have for your prayer life?

Read Ecclesiastes 3:1–8; and 8:5–7.

What role does wisdom play in God's sense of timing?

Read John 2:1–4; 7:6–8, 30; 13:1; 17:1.

Jesus, being both God and man, knew God's sense of timing. God works in perfect time, not just about the right time, or just missed the right time, but in perfect time. It is comforting for us to realize God is working all things in our lives at just the right time. Have you ever thanked God for that? That may mean thanking Him for not giving you what you've asked for, because in His wisdom, He understands you or someone else near you may not be ready for that yet. Problems arise when we expect things to happen before God's time, or we feel things should have happened (an untimely death for instance) after God's time. May we learn to trust God's judgment and timing.

3. Joy and Contentment

Read Galatians 5:22–26.

List the fruits of the Spirit.

1.

2.

3.

4.

5.

6.

7.

8.

9.

It's easy to live with these fruits when things are going well, but to live with these fruits when we have a painful experience in our lives, or when things aren't going the way we planned, is a little more difficult. That is when it is especially important for us to be in the Word and in prayer for the Holy Spirit to be working through us and giving us these fruits in abundance.

Paul tells us that to live by the fruits of the Spirit we must do something. What must we do? (5:24)

_____

What passions or evil desires do you need to learn to control in order to obtain the fruits of the Spirit? For instance, if you have problems with your temper, no doubt you often lack patience, gentleness, and self-control. If you are prone to overdrinking, you may be looking to alcohol for your joy and peace, and once again, lack self-control. If you sever relationships when you feel hurt, instead of forgiving, you lack faithfulness. Consider your life and which of these fruits you are lacking.

What things does Paul tell us to stay away from? (5:26)

_____

Read John 15:9–11.

What must we do to have joy and fulfillment in our lives?

_____

Read Philippians 4:11–13.

What is the secret of being content in any and every situation? (vs. 13)

_____

That means Christ can fill the voids in our life and, with His help, we can be OK with our situation whatever the circumstances. We have been assured God will always provide us with what we need (Matthew 6:25–27). Many of the other things we think we need are just things we want.

When my oldest daughter was just about two and about to start swimming lessons, I realized I didn't have a swimming suit for her. Within a few days, my husband came home from work with a box of clothes from a co-worker, and you guessed it, there were three swimming suits that were her size in the box. Contentment is being thrilled with the three suits that were provided regardless of if they were the color or style I would have chosen.

God provides for us in many ways, but sometimes we don't want what God provides because it doesn't meet our specifications or expectations. We so often lust for more or better things and covet and want what other people have. Lust, greed and jealousy come from the devil, the world, and our sinful nature. In Christ, we can find fullness and contentment...even when all our ideals aren't being met.

The Israelites weren't thrilled with manna. They would have preferred meat, potatoes and caramel apples. God determined that manna would provide sustainance, and would teach His children to trust.

Read 1 Timothy 6:6–10.

Paul says godliness with contentment is great gain. He's implying we don't start out there; in fact, it is a long spiritual step to get there. It is great gain to be content.

What is Paul's view of life that allows him to be content? (6:7, 8)

_____

How does that impact your life right now? What are you saving money for or spending money on that isn't a necessity? What are your financial goals? Do they fall in line with what you need? Most of us have much more than we need. Is it important for you to be spending your time at work? Are we working for necessities or for cable TV, a new house, a nice car, and vacations? Will those things lead us closer or further from Christ? Is our career about providing necessities or boosting our ego? Things can never bring happiness. In fact, as we've already learned, Christ is the only one who can bring happiness and contentment. Many people with lots of money are lonely, sad, bitter, and depressed. A good dose of contentment would have many of us living differently than we are living now.

Are you one of those people? Pray for the wisdom to live your life with contentment, and to have the same priorities for your life that God has.

4. Jealousy

Read 1 Corinthians 3:3 and 2 Corinthians 12:20.

List the worldly attributes Paul writes about and contrast them to the fruits of the Spirit.

_____

_____

You can live your life quarreling with your husband, children, friends and neighbors or you can live a life of love. Your life can be marked with outbursts of anger or joy. You can divide people into factions or promote peace, talk behind people's back and ruin reputations or be a faithful, kind friend. Your life can be marked by arrogance and disorder or goodness and self-control. You will either hurt and tear down or build up and encourage, depending on the fruit your life produces.

Read 1 Corinthians 3:16-17.

What significance is it that we are God's temple, especially in regards to jealousy?

_____

Isn't it true that if we are the temple of Christ, our actions will portray Christ to others? The fruits of the Spirit should be the sign of our life. Note verse 17. God will deal with those who put us down when we are living as the temple of Christ. We also ought to make sure we aren't putting others down who are living as the temple of Christ, or God just may deal with us.

Prayer to close the lesson:

Holy Father, open my eyes to the sins in my life that cause me the most pain. Give me the strength and determination to eliminate these things from my life. May doing so be a blessing to me and those around me. Protect my relationships with my family. Where there is discord, heal the pain and reconnect our lives. Let my life portray Christ to others. Help me to use the gifts You have given me to serve You. Show me how to do this and open my eyes and my heart to opportunities in front of me. In the name of my Lord and Savior I pray. Amen.

LESSON FIVE: JOCHEBED

Topics for Further Study: Obedience, God's Plan for Us and Our Children, and A Mother's Role.

READ EXODUS 1:6–14, 22, AND 2:1–10.

Devotion: Have you ever wondered what it would be like to try to conceal a newborn? Years ago I heard the story of people from a Vietnamese village hiding from American troops during the Vietnam War. They took refuge in the river, under a bridge. When an infant started to cry and its mother could not quiet it, the father held it under the water until it died. In doing so, he saved the people of the village.

What did Jochebed go through in those months as she tried to keep Moses hidden? No doubt she spent very little time anywhere outside her home. She couldn't risk anyone discovering Moses. One mistake could cost his life.

As mothers we know the innate love we have for our babies and the lengths we go to in order to ensure their safety. When it became impossible to hide Moses any longer, Jochebed acted in faith. In faith, and no doubt as a result of months of fervent prayer, Jochebed trusted that God would let the right person find her baby floating among the reeds.

How ironic that Pharaoh's daughter took pity on the baby and disobeyed her father's orders. This is a perfect example of God's ability to work in any situation and through any person. God had a plan for Moses, and a great one at that. Remember, God appeared to Moses and talked with him face to face, God buried Moses himself, and when Jesus revealed His glory to the disciples at the transfiguration, Moses and Elijah appeared with Him. It was God's plan that Pharaoh's daughter would rescue this tiny infant, the finest teachers in the land would educate him, and that he would know the goings-on of the court of Pharaoh.

When Moses' mother acted in faith, God rewarded her. Not only was she allowed to take Moses home and care for him, she was paid to do it, and with Pharaoh's money! In the time she nursed Moses, his mother was able to instill Hebrew values in him.

Jochebed's life illustrated the Christian principle that, "The earth is the Lord's and everything in it, the world, and all who live in it" (Psalm 24:1). We find such pleasure in ownership; of our cars, houses, and children. If we believe the above passage, we recognize that our children are first and foremost God's children. In only a few years, Jochebed impacted Moses' life in a way that instilled in him a deep sense of belonging to the Hebrew culture, despite his many years in Pharaoh's care.

It is important for mothers to note how our relationships with God make an impact on our children, even in their first few years of life. When we struggle with our young children in church, our determination to come week after week shows our dedication to worship. When family prayer and devotion time is a daily routine, children as young as two and three learn to communicate with God. Prayers before meals teach our children that our food and all we have is from God. What a beautiful responsibility Christian mothers have! Our greatest job is to carry the Word of God to the next generation, regardless of the other occupation we may have. Remembering that, we need to prioritize our life accordingly, making sure we take time each day to proclaim God's glory, power, and mercy. None of us knows what our futures or our children's futures hold, but equipping them with the tools of prayer, and reading God's Word that they might know Him, is equipping them for spiritual success and the benefits of eternal life.

As Christian mothers, our main goal is to bring up children to believe in their Savior so that we may spend eternity together. If our goal is worldly success, our priorities will be completely different. We won't worry about devotions at night nearly so much as our time is spent working on reading or math skills, or making sure they're on a good sports team. Vacation Bible school, Sunday school and youth group won't be a priority. We won't teach them the benefits of charitable giving, because our lives will illustrate that saving is more important, and that the neighbors and their hardships are too bad, but we have a new car and house and a whole list of other things that consume our money.

Perhaps the hardest lesson to teach our children is obedience to God's will. Every mother knows that obedience is a difficult value to instill in our children. Our children are often too selfish and rebellious to obey our wishes. If we aren't careful, the same can be true of us obeying God. The unexpected pregnancy in our life is easily misconstrued in our own minds as an obvious disruption of our lives instead of the miraculous blessing that it is. It is also God asking us to continue in our role as a mother, despite the well-meaning plans we've made for our future. The new neighbors whose kids are always running through our grass and are outside making noise way past our kids' bedtimes are rarely seen as the mission opportunity that they are.

Obedience to God often carries difficulty, challenge, and sometimes, even persecution. If we let our own emotions govern our lives, we may be in opposition and rebellion to God's choice of direction for us. Teaching our children to obey us without dissent, even when and if it isn't what they want to do, is a good lesson in learning how to obey their heavenly Father's calling in their lives. If they learn to listen to Him, they may find they're headed for a different career then they had planned, or to go to a college other than their first choice. It is also almost impossible without help from the Lord.

Despite the pain Jochebed endured in giving up Moses, God's blessings were certainly apparent with Moses later in life and with her other adult children. Aaron became the first priest of the Israelites (Exodus 28:1), and all the other priests were descendants of him. He was eloquent in speech, appointed to be God's mouthpiece to Pharaoh.

Miriam played a key role in the Exodus from Egypt and in leading the children of Israel to the Promised Land. In fact, she is the first woman in the Bible to display a role of leadership (Micah 6:4). We see God's hand preparing her for this role at a young age, when she was given the important responsibility of watching her baby brother floating among the reeds. No doubt she had been a significant help to her mother in the months of hiding Moses. Her praise after crossing the Red Sea was spontaneous, but shows a heart trained to give thanks to God.

Whenever we have a seemingly insurmountable task, whether it is potty training a child that doesn't seem to get it, a child that won't behave at bedtime, sit through church, or do his homework, we would do well to consider Jochebed. She had thousands of people who were supposed to throw her child in the river if they saw him. In faith, she trusted God to deliver her from that situation and God did. We need to remember that what is impossible with man is always possible with God.

Raising children is not easy, but look at this woman of the Bible. May we prioritize our lives as she did, that we, too, through trust and with prayer, may bring up men and women of God.

Devotion Question: Think about Jochebed's situation. She must have been elated when she was allowed to take Moses home to take care of him. But think about the day she took him to live in a heathen palace. A lot of people would say, there's just no hope for him, he'll see and hear too much evil. He won't know or remember God's ways. What does this lesson show us about the power of God to pervade any situation? What do you think Jochebed prayed for

Moses all those years while he was in the palace? What does that tell you about the years when your children are teens and seem unreachable? Who can reach them?

Topics for Further Study:

1. **Obedience**

Moses' mother obeyed God's law above the law of the Pharaoh and took extraordinary measures to ensure her child lived.

Read Isaiah 1:2–4, 15, 18–20.

What does God say about obedience in these passages?

_____

Read Exodus 1:15–21.

What blessing did the midwives receive from God as a result of their obedience?

_____

Read 1 Peter 1:13–15, 2:1–3.

How does "prepar[ing] your minds for action" contribute to us being obedient children of God?

_____

_____

What sort of ignorance is Peter talking about in verse 14?

_____

Peter says to seek holiness and crave pure spiritual milk. What is he trying to show with the illustration of babies craving pure spiritual milk? (Take notice of how often newborn babies eat!)

_____

Peter adds incentive at the end when he says, "Now that you have tasted that the Lord is good" (2:3). How does that tie into the Isaiah passage (1:19)?

_____

Read John 14:23, 24.

How can we know Jesus' teaching in order to obey it?

_____

Read 2 John: 5, 6.

John's writing sounds a bit cyclical. If you love God you obey His command and His command is to love. Jesus said, "'Love the Lord your God with all your heart and with all your soul and with all your mind.' This is the first and greatest commandment. And the second is like it: 'Love your neighbor as yourself'" (Matthew 22:37–39). Whole and very good books have been written on this subject.[9]

To walk in love is to walk the way Christ walked during His days on earth. He had compassion on the crowds; he healed the sick, forgave people's sins, fed the weary, and saved those on the brink of death. You might be asking how you can do those things today. You may not be able to heal the sick, but you can pray for God to heal the sick. Only God can forgive sins, but you can pray for someone to turn to repentance. You can forgive those who have harmed you. If Jesus commanded us to love, then a big part of obedience is the condition of our heart. If we are not full of love for all those God has put in our lives, then we are not obeying Jesus. To not obey is to walk in rebellion. Consider your feelings toward everyone in your life, from your family to your neighbors, etc. Are you being obedient to God's will?

2. God's Plan for Us and Our Children

Read Jeremiah 1:5–12, 17–19.

When did God design you?

_____

Look at Jeremiah 1:9.

Is there a particular time in your life when you realized you had a talent for something? What do you suppose God would have you do with that talent?

_____

What has God appointed you to do?

_____

If you are a Christian mother, He has appointed you to take

care of your children. You may be saying, "Then why didn't he give me patience, or a heart for dealing with young children?" The Lord made it clear to Jeremiah he didn't want to hear excuses. If God is with you, you can take God's words to Jeremiah to heart. "They will fight against you but will not overcome you, for I am with you and will rescue you" (Jeremiah 1:19).

"They" are the forces that keep you discontent being at home: the devil, the world, and your sinful nature. "They" are the stressors that make you think you are going to lose your mind after spending two days with your children. "They" are the excuses within you that say it's OK to keep yelling at your children instead of using a calm, loving voice and finding good, solid forms of discipline to replace yelling.

If you are married, God has also appointed you to be a helper to your husband. In a good marriage, a husband helps his wife plenty, too, but even if he doesn't, God doesn't need to hear all the reasons and excuses why it can't or won't work with your husband, or why his temper, or biting remarks, or inability to acknowledge how much you do for him, keep you from serving your husband. God has given you the tools and He is with you to rescue you when your husband isn't all you need him to be. Chances are you are not all your husband hoped or dreamed of either, because neither of you is perfect. Instead of turning to food, or a bottle of beer, or wine, or whatever, how about turning to the Lord for the strength to do the things you have been appointed to do? Have you prayed about and given God the impossible situations in your life that you haven't been able to solve?

Some women have been appointed to work outside the home, because of circumstances that make it impossible for them to stay home. If that is the case, the Lord has no doubt provided the means for you to have your children well taken care of. You are to be an example of a godly woman in the workplace, and a godly mother when you set foot inside the door of your home. Look to God to rescue you when you feel overwhelmed and out of patience, and make time in your day to be what your children need you to be, even if that means sacrificing a clean home, or some leisure reading time for yourself before bed.

Consider now what God has called you to be and to do, and put it down.

God appointed me to

_____.

What talents did God give you to accomplish what He appointed you to do?

_____

What do you need to ask God to supply for you to serve better in your appointed role?

_____

Read Jeremiah 29:11–13.

What must we do to find God?

_____

God says His plans are to prosper us, not to harm us, to give us a hope and a future. Why is it when we make godly choices, often we're the ones who are left without a lot of money to live on now, or to put away for retirement? Sometimes we are the ones who suffer the loss of a child or parent. This seems contrary to what God is saying to us. The fact is, God does work things out for our good (Romans 8:28), but that doesn't mean things go perfectly for us all the time. Jesus said, "In this world you will have trouble" (John 16:33). We can expect trouble, but we can also expect God to provide for us and to give us all we need during those times. David said in Psalm 37:25, "I was young and now I am old, yet I have never seen the righteous forsaken or their children begging bread." During the hardest times of my life, God has always surrounded me with blessings: a thoughtful neighbor or person from the church who stopped by to bring a meal or plate of cookies, a friend who wrote a note to tell me she was praying for me, someone who dropped by with a bag of clothes or toys or books for my children. God has always provided for me spiritually as well as physically. The same is true for you if you commit your life to Him. You may not end up the richest person on the block, but you will prosper. God's blessings are not just material. His blessings arrive in beautiful and healthy children, in a garden that produces abundantly, a fulfilling marriage, contentment, a husband who likes his job, and many more priceless things. Even when God doesn't give us perfectly healthy children, or a job our husband likes, He provides blessings to help us endure. He gives us the fruit of His Spirit: love, joy, peace, patience, kindness, goodness, faithfulness, gentleness, and self-control (Galatians 5:22). When God blesses us, He doesn't skimp. His hope is an eternal hope, and the life He prepares for us in heaven is the true reward for following Him while we're here on earth. If Jeremiah had not listened to the Lord, but had only said what the people wanted to hear or the things he wanted to say, would there be a book of Jeremiah in the Bible for you to read today? If we do not bring our children up to obey and know the Word of God, will they be able to fill the role and live in the blessings God has planned for them?

3. A Mother's Role

Read Titus 2:3–5. Note the nine attributes of a Christian woman (four from verse 3, one from verse 4, and four from verse 5).

1.

2.

3.

4.

5.

6.

7.

8.

9.

Look at the characteristics of a young Christian wife and mother. She is to love her husband and children, to be self-controlled, pure, to be busy at home, to be kind and subject to her husband. That's kind of a tall order, isn't it? When I think of women of the previous generation who I want to emulate, these were the characteristics they possessed. These are also the qualities I want to have while raising my family. I want them to think of me as kind and loving, and doing my work at home faithfully and loving my husband enough to say, "This is what I think, but you're the head of this house and if you think this is what God would want for us, then I trust your judgment." By doing that, I'm respecting my husband, but also asking him to bring God into the equation. Is it unbelievable to think God would ask a modern day woman to be subject to her husband?

Satan will do anything to assure you that the Bible is outdated and has no relevance to you today. Do you know why? Because the Bible is power and Satan doesn't want you to get it. God's Word has the power to stifle Satan. Jesus used it when He was being tempted. By the Word of God, the entire earth was made. By the word of Jesus, people came out of graves, the blind saw, the sea calmed. Why should you be subject to your husband? Because it works. God gave us a model for marriage that works if it is properly adhered to.

I have no statistic to back this up, but contrary to popular opinion, I think a high percentage of men suffer from feeling inadequate. Because they are men, they aren't going to say anything about it, but you'll catch on to it when you hear statements like, "I wish I could afford to get you that" or, "I just don't do much right, do I?" as an answer when you confront your husband about something. Why is it important to be subject to and submit and respect? Because if you nag and domineer and challenge his every decision, he will have no self-esteem and he'll lash out at you. If you give him the right to make decisions, then stand by him whether it goes well or not so well, he will love you. And isn't that what you want, even more than being right? I've fallen into the trap of treating my husband poorly on many occasions and it always backfires. If I bite my tongue, and go to the Lord in prayer, the result is so much better.

The Bible assures us we are all equal before the Lord. If you doubt, go back to Lesson Three and re-read the part on favoritism. Submitting does not make you less of a person. It's exactly what you do at work. You submit to your boss. You submit to the authorities in your town and state and country. That doesn't make you less equal. It makes you obedient. Submitting to your husband doesn't make you less equal than him either.

Besides the benefits we will reap from living that way, why else is it important that we live that way? (Titus 2:5)

_____

Read 1 Timothy 5:11–15.

What point is Paul making?

_____

Have you ever considered the many things you have to do at home actually keep you from sinning, or that it is a God-pleasing thing to keep a house and take care of your children and husband?

_____

Read Proverbs 31:26–30.

What attributes does a Christian mother possess? (two from verse 26, two from verse 27, and one from verse 30)

1.

2.

3.

4.

5.

The last one is the most important. If you are a woman who fears the Lord, all the other things will fall in line.

Prayer to close the lesson:

Holy Father in heaven, thank You for richly providing for me in every situation. I praise You that You have not left me floating in the middle of the river of life. Just as You had a plan for Moses, I know You have a plan for me as well. Keep my eyes on You when I feel like I am drowning. Direct the steps of my life that I can be what You made me to be. Give me all that I need to be the mother You created me to be, and the wife I should be. Forgive my past mistakes and give me the grace to do better in the future. In Jesus' name I pray. Amen.

Lesson Six: Manoah's Wife

Topics for Further Study: Guiding Our Husbands, When Children Fall Away, and The Christian Lifestyle

READ JUDGES 13; 14:1–4; 16:31.

Devotion: God again chose a childless couple to bear a son who would lead Israel. We've seen that in the case of Rachel's son Joseph, now Samson, and later Samuel and John the Baptist. These children could be attributed to nothing but a miracle of God. Born long before in-vitro fertilization, and in the case of Elizabeth, after child-bearing was physically possible, there could be no doubt in the parents' minds, or ours, that these children came directly from God.

The angel of the Lord announced the coming of this child. The angel would never have spoken to Manoah if it weren't for him asking the angel to reappear, because the angel's instruction were for Manoah's wife, as she would bear Samson and take care of him. Since our focus is mothers, we won't look at Manoah, except to make one point. Though Manoah had questions, he didn't doubt what the angel of the Lord said. He believed his wife, and more importantly, he trusted the words of the angel of the Lord. In his prayer, he said, "Teach us to bring up the boy *who is to be born*" (Judges 13:8), and to the Lord asked, "*When your words are fulfilled*, what is the rule of the boy's life and work?" (13:12). What unswerving faith to believe and not question what was to come, but only to ask for guidance in how to deal with the gift God was about to give!

Notice how Manoah's wife stayed calm, then calmed Manoah when the angel of the Lord ascended in the flame. We should strive to have the same effect on our husbands. Our reaction to any and all situations can lead our husbands to take the godly path. Wise and careful words at the right time can diffuse anger, clarify confusion, comfort hurt, and divert disappointment. [10] What an awesome privilege we have! Only through daily prayer and Bible study, and with and through the help of the Holy Spirit, can we stand up to such responsibility. If we offer our husbands worldly wisdom, such as urging them to do what feels good or makes them happy, telling them they deserve better in a certain situation, or anything else contrary to what God says in His Word, we won't lull our husbands into calm, but will lead them to greater turmoil and down the path of sin.

As we skip ahead to the point in Samson's life when he is looking for a wife, an interesting scenario unfolds. Samson's parents rightly tried to talk Samson into marrying a godly spouse. That is what the Bible tells Christians to do (Genesis 24:3, Ezra 9:2, I Corinthians 7:39, 2 Corinthians 6:14, Ephesians 5:11), and what most of us would hope for our children. But we see God using Samson's obstinate behavior to accomplish what He had sent him for. Just as with Jacob's messy life, we see God working in, around and through Samson's weaknesses.

1 Corinthians 13:12 states, "Now we see but a poor reflection as in a mirror; then we shall see face to face. Now I know in part; then I shall know fully, even as I am fully known." Sometimes we don't understand or approve the direction our children take. If their faith is still intact and if we are praying regularly for our children, we can be confident in God's hand to make their less than ideal choices and decisions work for His kingdom.

Perhaps the sport they are led to play was really about them meeting the Christian friend who will help them through tough times, or be a guiding influence on them. Maybe it is God's hand guiding them to someone who needs to know the Lord. Perhaps the family of your child's future spouse needs a Christian influence in their life. Maybe the lesson they learn now will impact the rest of their life.

That is not to say children can't fall away or make poor decisions. Even we are capable of that! However, when our children remain in the Lord and in His Word and are open to His discipline and redirection, we can be confident in God's grace. God inspired the writer of Judges to pen the words in 14:4: "His parents did not know that this was from the Lord, who was seeking an occasion to confront the Philistines; for at the time they were ruling over Israel." Often in times of trouble or conflict, God is working in our lives for our good, or in Samson's case, to accomplish what He had for him to do.

Children are a gift from God, and God chose the children that are right for you. If you have lamented a time or two over your child's stubbornness, or strong will, or perhaps lack of ambition, you can be assured the characteristics of your child are fitting for the purpose God had in mind when he created them. God gave Samson unyielding strength; he was obstinate and stubborn. When Samson's former fiancée was given to his best friend, Samson caught three hundred foxes and started their tails on fire, setting them loose to destroy the Philistine's crops. Another person might have spent a year crying, or left the country for a few weeks. God created Samson to bring Israel out of the hands of the Philistines.

Those same characteristics that God gave Samson in order to save Israel from the Philistines led to his downfall. Instead of being obstinate and stubborn and unwilling to yield to Satan and his deceptions, Samson rebelled against God's ways and fell into sin. Even when our children reject godly counsel from us and stray from the Lord, our prayers can never cease for them to return to the Lord, and we must stand firm in God's ways, instead of falling into the trap of acceptance. Jesus said, "Anyone who loves his son or daughter more than me is not worthy of me" (Matthew 10:37). Good Christian men and women who live according to God's standards often break down and accept their adult child's behavior. Some parents accept and excuse divorces that aren't Biblical, a child's drinking or spending problem, and adult children's career ambitions that lead them to neglect to take care of their own families. Sometimes parents are willing to accept these things in the name of keeping the peace, instead of confronting in a loving manner the child and their sins, in hope of turning them from sin.

Some parents go so far as to boast of their children's deviation from the scripture; they speak well of their children's high paying career that leaves little time for their children and less time to serve at church. Parents rejoice that a child who was living with their boy/girlfriend finally got married, but if the person the child married is an unbeliever there may be little to celebrate. Paul warns if we must boast, "Boast in the Lord. For it is not the one who commends himself who is approved, but the one whom the Lord commends" (2 Corinthians 10:17-18). As parents we have to work hard to not give a nod of approval for worldly gain that leaves spiritual bankruptcy.

Becoming a parent is an awesome responsibility. Being a Christian parent requires even more commitment. God tells us in Jeremiah 1:5, "Before I formed you in the womb I knew you, before you were born I set you apart." God blesses our children with attributes to accomplish His will, but if we, and our children, aren't obedient, we will not make progress for the kingdom of heaven. Manoah and his wife obeyed God and believed in His decision to give them Samson. They tried to keep Samson under control and to direct him back to the ways of the Lord. By doing so, they opened themselves up to receive other blessings. God blessed this woman, previously referred to as sterile, with other children (Judges 16:31).

God knew what He was doing when He wove us in our mothers' wombs and our children in ours. He will strengthen and provide for us when it comes to caring for our husbands and children, and we would do well to be obedient to Him and His ways.

Devotion Question: What sins do you approve of, consciously or subconsciously? Are you attached to a TV program that flaunts an ungodly lifestyle? Do you find yourself complaining to your husband often? Do you love to spread the latest gossip without concern for the person the gossip is about? Do you look for the way you benefit in every situation instead of considering how the Lord is working not just for your good, but the good of the other people involved? Take some time and examine your life to see if sin has taken hold of you in any area of your life. Then pray about these things and make a real effort to change them.

Topics for Further Study:

1. **Guiding Our Husbands**

Read Esther 4:1–5:8; 7:1–4; and 9:11–13.

Once Esther realized she had to get involved and she also had to involve the king, what did she do?

_____

What should be our first step in all matters, whether dealing with our husbands or not?

Can you imagine not eating or drinking anything for three days? In our culture and in our day that is unheard of. If we miss a meal we are sure to make up for it at the next. What did this fasting by the entire population of the Jews show?

_____

Why didn't Esther say anything to Xerxes at the first banquet?

_____

Have you noticed how crucial timing is in your relationships? How often do you unload your problems on your husband as soon as he walks in the door from a long day at work? When do your best conversations with your husband occur?

_____

What does Esther teach us about timing?

_____

Look again at Esther 9:11–13. Of what benefit was it to Esther to act as she did?

_____

Esther was working on God's time and in God's way. As Christian women, we will go much farther with our husbands if we involve God and act in His time, which we learned is always perfect.

Read Mark 6:17–29.

How did Herodias deal with her first husband?

_____

Why didn't Herod kill John initially instead of just having him put in prison?

_____

On what day of the year did Herodias make her request through her daughter? (verse 21)

How did Herod feel about the request? (verse 26)

Herodias and Esther show stark contrasts in the way they dealt with their husbands. Esther was gentle, but strong, patient, and submissive. Esther chose her words carefully. She called Xerxes "king" and "your majesty." She was his wife and in her language gave him every honor. Herodias took advantage of the king and stepped all over his desires in order to get what she wanted. Both women got what they wanted, but Herod was deeply distressed, while Xerxes came back to Esther and sought further advice from her.

How do you treat your husband? The strength of showing respect to your husband is that it often leads a husband to seek your advice. When you treat him kindly, he will come back to you. I doubt Herod's relationship with Herodias was anything but cold for quite some time after John's death.

2. When Children Fall Away

We did not read the entire account of Samson, but if we had, we would see he had a weakness for women, and indeed it was a woman, and the sins incurred from his love of her, that brought about his demise. The Lord did return to Samson in the hour of his death.

Read Proverbs 22:6.

This passage gives us the first step in keeping our children from falling away. What is it and how do we do it?

_____

Read Deuteronomy 6:6–9. The way you live your life is going to be one of the biggest influences on your child's life. Taking them to Sunday school once a week will not teach them to live a godly life. It is a start, but if we go to church, then come home and watch TV shows that show people living contrary to God's way, and curse at our children, and think and say the worst about other people, chances are our children will live like we live the six days of the week we aren't at church. Moses tells us to talk about God's ways all day, every day, and have reminders about God in our houses and all around us.

_____

_____

Read Ezekiel 34:15–16; Matthew 18:12–14; and Luke 15:7.

What is God the Father's heart toward His children who are wandering from His ways?

_____

_____

Read Matthew 18:14, 18–20.

This serves as a guide for how to pray for children who are

falling away or who have already fallen. What three specific things can we use as a guide for our prayer life?

_____

From verse 14:

_____

From verse 18:

_____

From verse 19:

_____

_____

It is always encouraging when you know beyond a shadow of a doubt that what you are praying for is in accordance with God's will. Jesus assures us that when we pray for a child who is straying to return to God, we are praying what is God's will.

It is important that we don't just pray for the circumstances; that is, for a child to quit drinking or doing drugs, or whatever it may be that has led them astray. We need to pray for those things for sure, but Jesus tells us to bind them to heaven and to pray for their souls. In Matthew 10:28, Jesus said, "Do not be afraid of those who kill the body, but cannot kill the soul. Rather, be afraid of the One who can destroy both soul and body in hell."

Jesus tells us not to worry about physical death as long as we, and our children, are walking with the Lord, because we will inherit eternal life. He says to pray earnestly, day and night without ceasing, for the child who has denounced their faith, and pray their life is spared so they can return to the Lord.

And finally, Jesus tells us to join forces with other Christians. Swallow your pride and ask others to pray for your straying child.

Read Matthew 10:37–39.

Perhaps the hardest part of a child straying is the temptation to overlook the sin in order to keep your relationship with your child. Jesus tells us if we love our son or daughter more than Him, we are not worthy of Him.

Paul says in 1 Corinthians to "hand this man over to Satan, so that the sinful nature may be destroyed and his spirit saved on the day of the Lord" (5:5). That means sometimes a person needs to spend a season with the devil. In the parable of the prodigal son, the son left the father and squandered all his inheritance. The father did not seek his son, bring him home, and watch his son go out each night to live wildly. It is of utmost importance that our children understand our love is unconditional. But, it is equally important that our child understand that, "We must obey God rather than men" (Acts 5:29). That may mean a holiday or two without the child if they insist on bringing the man or woman they are living with who had a spouse and a child or two before meeting our child. It may mean your child refuses your invitation to dinner because you told him his life of gambling had to stop before it destroyed him. It will certainly mean you will bear a cross, and a heavy one at that. To do anything different, Jesus says, makes you unworthy of Him.

3. The Christian Lifestyle

Read 1 Corinthians 12:12–31.

If you are a Christian, what is your identity? You are a part of what? (verse 27)

_____

What role, if any, do you have in your church?

_____

Are you comfortable with the role or lack of a role?

_____

If you are a believer in Christ and therefore a part of the body of Christ, you should be doing something for the body of Christ. Just as each different part of your physical body plays a key role in your existence, you were designed to play a key role in your church. Next time an announcement is made in church seeking volunteers to do something, consider doing it. We are all busy, and you don't have to volunteer to do everything. If everyone volunteered a little, we would all be doing a little and accomplishing a lot! I cannot play the organ, but I have asked the organist to baby-sit for a Mother's Bible study. The organist's job is to play the organ, but no one else volunteered to baby-sit. That's like asking your ear to lift up a pencil, because your hand isn't interested. An important part of leading a

Christian lifestyle is examining how much time you are giving the Lord. If you hardly know people at church, except the people who teach your child's Sunday school class, it's time to get involved! Consider what you are able to do: bake, dish food at a pre-service fellowship hour or supper, be a helper for Sunday school, make banners, sing, pray, organize, clean. Someone is waiting for you to say, "I'm pretty good at such and such, would you like some help?"

Read 1 Thessalonians 4:11-12.

Paul tells us to lead a quiet life. What does that mean?

_____

What other benefits are there to staying busy (verse 12)?

_____

Read Ephesians 5:15–21.

List ten attributes of a Christian lifestyle.

1. (verse 15)

2. (verse 16)

3. (verse 17)

4. (verse 17)

5. (verse 18)

6. (verse 18)

7. (verse 19)

8. (verse 19)

9. (verse 20)

10. (verse 21)

Which ones do you need to work on?

_____

If you have these things down, help your fellow Christian women. Encourage them to do the same and pray for them.

Prayer to close the lesson:

Heavenly Father, thank You for the children You gave me and for their unique traits that set them apart to do Your will. Help me to bring them up in Your ways so they can reach their full potential to serve You. Give me wisdom when dealing with my husband. Let my life be a reflection of Your ways. Change the traits in me that cause my husband to stray. Let my life glorify You, as Jesus glorified You with His life on earth. In our Savior's name we pray. Amen.

Lesson Seven: Hannah

Topics for Further Study: Prayer, Oaths, and Blessings and Curses

READ 1 SAMUEL 1 AND 2:19–21.

Devotion: Hannah was a troubled woman. As with any unchecked sin, polygamy and the consequences of it made Hannah's life miserable. Her being barren would have been much more tolerable had she not had to contend with Peninnah and her children.

The Lord decided not to give Hannah children. In verse 5 we read, "The Lord had closed her womb." Samuel 1:7 says, "This went on year after year," leading us to believe that Hannah suffered with this burden for some length of time.

Hannah's husband, Elkanah, appears to have been a reverent man. He went regularly to make his yearly offering at the temple, and when Hannah made a promise to God, he made sure she kept it. But he doesn't seem to be a great comfort to his wife in the midst of her suffering. When she cried at Peninnah's cruel taunting, his response was, "Hannah, why are you weeping? Why don't you eat?

Why are you downhearted? Don't I mean more to you than ten sons?" (1:8).

Eat, he says, why cry; after all, you've got me. Elkanah didn't get it. What did food mean to Hannah when she didn't have a child? As much as Hannah's husband no doubt meant to her, he couldn't fill the pain and frustration and longing for a child within her. Not only did Hannah suffer; she suffered alone. Even when she went before God to pour her heart out at the temple, Eli accused her of being drunk.

How often have we been in Hannah's shoes, in great distress over something in our lives, with all the people around us unable to understand? Add in a scoffer like Peninnah or an accuser like Eli and the misery just doesn't seem to end.

Hannah showed us exactly what to do in times like that. "In bitterness of soul Hannah wept much and prayed to the Lord" (1:10). And to Eli she said, "I am a woman deeply troubled…I was pouring out my soul to the Lord…I have been praying here out of my great anguish and grief"(1:15, 16).

Even when those closest to us can't relate to our problems, we have an ever-present help a prayer away. Psalm 34:18 says, "The Lord is close to the brokenhearted and saves those who are crushed in spirit." Later in the Psalms we read, "[The Lord] heals the brokenhearted and binds up their wounds. He determines the number of stars and calls each by name. Great is our Lord and mighty in power; his understanding has no limit" (Psalm 147:3-5). What a comfort! It doesn't matter if our family or friends or even our husbands understand what we are going through. Because God knows the thoughts and feelings of everyone involved, He understands us and our situation more than even we do. It is an awesome concept to try to fathom that God's understanding has no limit. Why do we spend so much of our time seeking the advice of people with limited understanding, when we have access to God?

When Paul pleaded with God to remove the thorn in his side, God responded by saying, "My grace is sufficient for you, for my power is made perfect in weakness" (2 Corinthians 12:9). What made God decide to "remember" Hannah, and give her what she asked, thereby removing the thorn in her side?

With great anguish, Hannah prayed to God and with an oath promised that if God gave her a son, she would give that child to God. Imagine doing what Hannah did. She carried a child in her womb and kept him just until he was weaned, then left him at the temple. This is reminiscent of Moses' mother, Jochebed, and also of Abraham being asked to sacrifice Isaac, the son he waited and longed for his whole life. God saw in Abraham and Hannah that their love for Him outweighed the love for these children—their only children. When Hannah prayed to God, she assured Him with her promise that His will and divine plan was more important than her earthly longings. With Paul, God saw that the thorn made Paul more willing and able to serve him; whereas Hannah was able to serve the Lord more by giving her son to be a prophet.

Eli's blessing of Hannah, both before and after she had Samuel, is noteworthy. Once he understood Hannah's situation, he told her to go in peace and added, "May the God of Israel grant you what you have asked of Him" (1 Samuel 1:17). He didn't know what it was she was troubled about or what she was asking God for. What a beautiful example to us. How often do we notice someone looking depressed or agitated, or even just worn out? We can go to the Lord on their behalf without prying into his or her life, and we can bless and encourage that person without knowing details.

After Samuel was dedicated to the Lord, Eli encouraged and blessed Elkanah and Hannah again that they would bear children to replace the one she gave to the Lord. And they did have more children, five more in fact, because, "The Lord was gracious to Hannah" (1 Samuel 2:21).

Devotion Question: Think again of Psalm 147:4-5, "[The Lord] determines the number of stars and calls each by name. Great is our Lord and mighty in power; his understanding has no limit." Do you ever find yourself praying and trying to explain a situation to the Lord? Or, do you offer solutions to your problems to the Lord?

For instance, have you asked God to give you a raise so you can pay off your debt? Have you ever considered doing that is assuming God doesn't understand the situation? You assume if He did understand, He would have already given you a raise, so you need to tell Him how your debt is likely to get paid. For some people, a raise would indeed do the trick, but if overspending is a problem, no amount of money could pay off debt you keep accumulating. Consider the way you pray, and consider the depth of this passage. Is your prayer life in need of some fine-tuning?

Topics for Further Study:

1. The Importance of Prayer

Read Deuteronomy 4:7; Psalm 34:15; Jeremiah 29:12-13.

Why should we pray?

_____

What does the Lord ask of us?

_____

Read Luke 18:1–7; Acts 1:14; Ephesians 6:18; and 1 Thessalonians 5:17.

How often should we pray?

_____

Read 1 Chronicles 5:18–20; Matthew 21:18–22; and James 5:13–18.

What attributes are important in praying?

From Chronicles—

From Matthew—

From James—

Using these passages for reference, when should we pray?

_____

Read Romans 1:17 and Romans 5:19.

How do we become righteous, like Elijah, so that our prayers are powerful and effective?

_____

_____

Read John 14:12–14; Romans 8:28; and 2 Corinthians 12:7–9.

After reading Jesus' words, how can we account for things we ask for in prayer and do not receive?

_____

_____

Did Jesus give any indication of the amount of time that should pass between when we ask of things and when we would receive them? How many things have you quit praying for if you didn't receive them in the first weeks, months, or even years after you asked?

Read Romans 8:26-27

What do we do when we are so upset we don't know how to pray?

_____

_____

Read Matthew 6:5–7; 1 Peter 3:7; and 1 Peter 4:7.

What should we not do when we pray?

_____

_____

Read Daniel 6:10; Jonah 2:1; Matthew 6:6; Matthew 26:39; and John 17:1.

I think it is interesting to see the different ways people prayed. Daniel prayed on his knees. Jonah was in the belly of the fish. Jesus said go in a private place; He prayed with His face to the ground, and standing with His hands toward heaven. That shows us we can pray at any time in any position. There are no limits to the way you pray, when you pray, or how you pray. What a comfort.

2. Oaths

Read Numbers 30.

Was Elkanah under an obligation to fulfill the oath Hannah made to God? (30:8) What does that tell you about Elkanah? After all, it was his son, too, that Hannah promised to give to the Lord.

_____

Read Joshua 9:14–25.

What did the men of Israel fail to do before making an oath? (9:14)

_____

_____

Why did they keep the oath, even if it was a foolish oath to make? (9:20)

_____

_____

Read Matthew 5:33–37.

What does Jesus say about oaths in general, and particularly to God?

_____

Do you ask your children to promise to do things? In light of what Jesus said, is that a wise thing to do?

_____

When is it good and right to make promises?

_____

_____

3. **Blessings and Curses**

Read Genesis 12:2–4.

Why would that make you think twice before uttering a word against someone?

_____

Read Numbers 22:1–12, 23:1–12, 24:9–13; and Deuteronomy 23:3–5.

Balaam was a pagan sorcerer hired to curse the Israelites. What ultimately would have been the result if he had cursed the Israelites on behalf of the Moabite king? (Numbers 24:9)

_____

Why didn't the Lord allow Balaam to curse Israel? (Numbers 22:12)

_____

_____

The Moabites were cursed by the Lord for what two reasons? (Deuteronomy 23:4)

_____

Read Joshua 24:9-10.

It's interesting to think of the people of Israel camped outside of Moab at the time Balak, the king of Moab, and Balaam were trying to curse them. Likely they had no idea someone was on a mountain above them trying to do them harm. This was somehow revealed to the people of Israel at a later time, and here, Joshua is reminding the people of this as a means of persuading them to not stray from following the Lord, but to put their trust in Him. What does this tell you about the people who may be trying to harm you, whether you know it or not?

_____

Read Malachi 2:2.

Have your blessings ever been a curse to you?

_____

_____

Read each of the following passages to discover how we set our hearts to honor God.

Numbers 20:12

Proverbs 3:9

Proverbs 14:31

Isaiah 29:13

1 Corinthians 6:18-20

Read Romans 12:14 and James 3:9–12.

As God's people, are we to curse anyone or anything?

_____

What are we to do instead?

_____

Read Galatians 3:13, 14.

How do we receive the same blessing God gave to Abraham?

_____

_____

If we have that same blessing, who can cause us harm with their words (curses)?

_____

Prayer to close the lesson:

Heavenly Father, thank You for the gift of prayer and the access that it gives me to You day or night. Forgive me for not always giving it the precedence in my life that it deserves. Too often I fail to really seek You with my whole heart until something goes wrong. Bless my mouth, Lord. Let my speech be full of grace and love and wisdom that comes from You. In Jesus' name. Amen

LESSON EIGHT: RIZPAH

Topics for Further Study: The Biblical View of a Mother's Love, Waiting on the Lord, and Perseverance

READ JOSHUA 9:3–14, 22–27; 1 SAMUEL 20:11–16; 2 SAMUEL 21:1–14.

Devotion: Rizpah was a woman who had to endure circumstance. Solomon said in Ecclesiastes 9:11, "The race is not to the swift or the battle to the strong, nor does food come to the wise or wealth to the brilliant or favor to the learned; but time and chance happen to them all." In other words, sometimes things just happen.

All of us know someone who has been struck by tragedy: a family member who died unexpectedly in the prime of life, a cancer-stricken friend or relative, a car accident that paralyzed a loved one, a child born with a disability or disease.

Sometimes these things happen. It doesn't mean those people are being punished, or that God somehow forgot to look after their loved ones. Jesus explained it to His disciples with this account: "As he went along, he saw a man blind from birth. His disciples asked him, 'Rabbi, who sinned, this man or his parents, that he was born blind?' 'Neither this man nor his parents sinned,' said Jesus, 'but this happened so that the work of God might be displayed in his life'" (John 9:1–3).

Again, on a different occasion, Jesus said, "Or those eighteen who died when the tower of Siloam fell on them--do you think they were more guilty than all the others living in Jerusalem? I tell you, no!" (Luke 13:4, 5).

Rizpah was one of Saul's concubines (2 Samuel 3:7), and as such, she gave birth to two of Saul's sons. Her place in life was in Saul's harem, and those children came to be because of it.

The note in one of my Bibles explains the Gibeonite "annihilation" this way. "Saul's action against the Gibeonites is not related elsewhere but appears to have been instituted early in his reign, motivated by an excessive nationalism (if not tribalism—the Gibeonites occupied territory partly assigned to Benjamin, and Saul's great-grandfather was known as the "father of Gibeon," 1 Chronicles 8:29; 9:35). [11]Saul's attack on the Gibeonites to restore land he felt rightfully belonged to his great-grandfather broke the oath Joshua made with the Gibeonites as a treaty of peace. In the lesson about Hannah, we learned it was better to not make an oath than to make an oath and break it. Joshua said breaking the oath would bring wrath upon the people (Joshua 9:20).

Saul's sin in carrying out this plot against the Gibeonites affected many people. First, there were the unsuspecting Gibeonites. The words "annihilate" (2 Samuel 21:2) and "decimated" (2 Samuel 21:5) lead us to believe many people were slaughtered, and those who were left survived to face the aftermath of a tragedy of that magnitude. Also, David and all the people of Israel were affected by the drought that struck the land as a response to this crime. And Rizpah, as well as Saul's daughter Merab, paid with the lives of their sons.

Whether we realize it or not, our sins typically affect other people. Certainly our immediate family bears the brunt of our weaknesses. Consider from this account that others: neighbors, friends, relatives, coworkers, and even the person driving next to us on the road, or the waitress when we go out to eat, or the person who answers the phone at a business office at your local utility company, can all be subject to the effects of our sins on a daily basis. Uncontrolled anger will ripple through all kinds of situations and turn itself on many unsuspecting people. Impatience will rear its ugliness in the grocery store line as easily as in our living rooms. Selfish thinking will consume us, allowing us to believe no one else is dealing with anything like us and will lead to intolerance at almost every level, from those we are closest to to anyone who crosses our path.

Consider how you want to affect those people with whom you come in contact. Do you want those people to see the uncontrolled sins in your life? Or would you rather be a reflection of God and His love? It is often the way we react when things do not go as they should that we have the best chance to demonstrate the fruits of the Spirit. Imagine the surprise and delight of the receptionist at your garbage company when, with patience and kindness and gentleness, you explain your bill is wrong for the third month in a row. What an unsuspected blessing when you are considerate to and of other drivers in the grocery store parking lot, even when you are dealing with sick kids at home. We can excuse rudeness easily enough. It was the third month and the third fifteen-minute call to the garbage company after all. You can always allow yourself to believe you don't have time to wait for that lady crossing the grocery store parking lot, and besides, you can squeeze by her with room to spare. Never mind that she stops and waits because she doesn't see it that way.

When we consider our speech and actions portray the condition of our hearts, we may have reason to confess we have indeed fallen short. Jesus said we are to be the light and salt of the world (Matthew 5:13, 14). We are a light when we demonstrate the fruits of the Spirit during those times the rest of the world would fall into sin. We are salt when our actions stand apart when and if we are the only one in that grocery store parking lot, or aisle, or checkout line to exhibit patience and perhaps even a word of encouragement or gratitude to the cashier and person bagging our groceries.

The question that arises is why did God wait to send the drought during David's reign? Since Saul killed the Gibeonites, why didn't God immediately quit sending rain on the land then?

Saul's heart was not like David's. Very early in his reign, Saul was rejected by God (1 Samuel 15:23). When God commanded Saul to do something, Saul always obeyed God somewhat, but in his own way. When Samuel told him to meet him for a sacrifice, Saul waited until the set day, and then impatiently burned the sacrifice himself, only to have Samuel arrive shortly after he took matters into his own hands (1 Samuel 13:10). When God told Saul, through Samuel, to completely destroy the Amalekites and everything they owned, Saul destroyed everyone and everything except the king and the best sheep, goats, and cattle (1 Samuel 15). The longer Saul reigned, the further he strayed from the Lord. More likely than not, God saw Saul wouldn't have had a change of heart for the sin he committed against the Gibeonites, but would have rebelled further against the Lord. Had Saul humbled himself and admitted his guilt, the Gibeonites likely wouldn't have had the opportunity to take Saul's sons.

As it was, God saw the plight of the Gibeonites and sought justice on their behalf. Unfortunately for her, Rizpah was mother to two of Saul's sons whose lives were demanded of them. She was the victim of circumstance. Her sons were killed and left on a hill like trash. What is a mother to do in such a situation?

This mother, who no doubt had done what she could to protect her sons during life, dedicated herself to doing the same thing in their death. Day and night she guarded her sons and the other five bodies until word came to the king, who had mercy on her and gave all seven of the men, plus Jonathon and Saul, proper burials.

Rizpah's plight illustrates the extent of a mother's love. Not every mother is good, but more often than not, a mother's love is a bond that is not easily shaken. It is what takes us to the foot of our children's bed at night when they're sick or scared. It is what takes us to our knees in prayer when they are hurting. It is what gets us up early in the morning to make sure they have the clothes and the lunch and the other things to start their day right. It brings forth a scream we never knew we had when we find our children on the edge of a dangerous situation. It is what puts us back in the delivery room in a pain unlike any other after we've done it once. It is what makes the pain fade the minute we see our children and hold them in our arms.

Rizpah's account also shows us that God does not turn away from us forever. Many days and nights, Rizpah must have felt alone and forsaken. Eventually her actions received the attention of the king himself. No matter what our position, be it very high in God's kingdom, or ever so low, we are never beyond God's visibility. Rizpah's actions are an example for us to persist in doing what is right. Merab wasn't out there, nor are we told of anyone keeping Rizpah company, but Rizpah persevered.

How often don't you feel all alone or way out on a limb with little or no support? Whether at home or at work, if you are doing what is right, then press on. Eventually your actions are bound to get the attention of the King, and His rewards are eternal.

Devotion Question: What sins do you easily fall prey to in regards to your everyday life and the example you are to other people? Are you considerate of your neighbors, other drivers, your children and husband?

Write down the areas you need to work on and pray to change your words and actions.

Topics for Further Study:

1. **The Biblical View of a Mother's Love**

   Read Isaiah 49:15-16 and Isaiah 66:13.

   What is a mother's love compared to in these passages?

   _____

   Read John 16:21.

   What other experience in life is like childbirth, going through pain and anguish and moments later being filled with joy?

   _____

   Read 1 Thessalonians 2:6–8.

   List the attributes of motherhood Paul uses in this illustration.

   _____

   _____

   _____

   Did you ever consider that by becoming a mom, God was equipping you with some of the very tools you need to minister to unbelievers?

   _____

   _____

Read Jeremiah 31:15 and Matthew 2:16–18.

If God's love is like a mother's love only more perfect and more intense, as we saw in the passages we read earlier from Isaiah, what does this passage tell you about those God has sought and called who leave Him and go to an eternal death, like Judas?

_____

_____

Read Isaiah 63:9 and Jeremiah 31:20.

What is God's sentiment toward us, His children?

_____

_____

How does God feel when He has to discipline us?

_____

_____

God's heart yearns for us and we are His delight. The way you feel about your children is the way God feels about you. It is an awesome thing to discover God goes through with us all the same things we go through with our children, only His judgment is never wrong, and His love is more intense and perfect. We fail in many ways and on many occasions, but God does not fail us. In the wee hours of the night when you pray over a sick child or you pray for a teenage son or daughter who is gone on a band trip, or even for an adult child who is straying from the Lord, you are not praying to someone who is detached and unaware of your distress. Isaiah wrote, "In all their distress he too was distressed" (Isaiah 63:9).

Sometimes as mothers we feel as if no one, not even our husbands, understand what we feel with our children, and it can be very lonely. God watches out for our children even when we can't. We have many limitations. We need sleep, and can only be in one place at a time. God doesn't need a break and our child is always in His sight. What a wonderful solace to us—and a great encouragement. What a gift He has given us with our capacity to love and nurture our children.

2. Waiting on the Lord

Read Psalm 37:7–11.

During trouble and hardship, what should we do?

_____

What should we not do?

_____

_____

Read Psalm 40:1 and Psalm 130:5–7.

What assurance do we have that good will come from waiting on the Lord?

_____

Read Isaiah 54:7, 8.

How long did the Lord turn away from His people?

_____

_____

How long does His kindness last?

_____

Read Isaiah 30:18.

What are the blessings of waiting on the Lord?

_____

Read Psalm 27:7–14

Write from these verses what David is asking the Lord to do for him.

From verse 7:

1.

2.

From verse 9:

1.

2.

From verse 11:

1.

2.

From verse 12:

1.

Who, besides the Lord, can we count on? (verse 10)

_____

What two things has God been to David that led him to write verse 14 with confidence? (verse 9)

_____

How is waiting on the Lord different than being patient?

_____

Patience is enduring suffering without complaining or calmly tolerating delay.[12] To wait is to remain, to be ready[13]. Being patient is the way that we are to wait…to calmly and without complaining wait (remain, be ready) for God to deliver us from our circumstances. Waiting on the Lord is to trust in God as our Redeemer and Savior who loves us with an unyielding love and to seek His solutions which often take considerably more time than ours because they deal with a change of heart, not just circumstances.

3. **Perseverance**

Read James 1:2–4, 12.

Of what benefit is perseverance to a Christian? (verse 4)

_____

_____

Read James 5:10–11.

What is James' definition of perseverance? (verse 10)

_____

_____

James 1:12 and James 5:11 call those who have persevered what?

_____

_____

What will the outcome of perseverance be?

_____

Read 1 Corinthians 13:7.

_____

What word is directly in front of perseveres?

_____

_____

If you use James' definition of perseverance and Paul's message that love always perseveres, what does that mean for the relationships in your life?

_____

_____

Many Christian women have cut off ties with their relatives (mother-in-law, aunts, cousins, etc). Paul says love always perseveres, so not persevering is not living in love, and not living in love is living apart from God. If we are to be totally honest, relationships with our own siblings, parents, and husband can be strained at times, but perseverance is to be patient during those times and to call on God to intervene, to change hopes, expectations, or attitudes, either ours or theirs.

What implications does Paul's definition of love have in regards to our marriages?

_____

_____

Read Hebrews 10:32–39.

What are some of the ways the Hebrews persevered? (verses 32–34)

_____

_____

What are some ways we persevere today?

_____

_____

What are we to have as we are persevering? (verse 35)

_____

What will cause God to not be pleased with us? (verse 38)

_____

Read Luke 8:15; Romans 5:3–4.

What attribute produces the crop?

_____

What else does perseverance produce?

_____

What a good thing to keep in the back of our minds when our children are experiencing trouble, hardship, or persecution at school, on the bus, or in the neighborhood. Perseverance produces character. God is in the process of molding our children into the people He needs them to be to use them for the rest of their lives.

_____

Read 2 Thessalonians 3:4-5.

Who are we modeling when we persevere?

_____

_____

Read 1 Timothy 4:16.

Why does it matter that we keep trying to be a Christian mother and Christian wife, and to persevere in difficult relationships?

_____

Read 2 Peter 1:5–9.

List the attributes we are to seek:

_____

What sort of effort are we to make to acquire these attributes? (verse 5)

_____

_____

If we do not persevere in disciplining our children and in showing love to our husbands, what do we become? (verse 8)

_____

Have you felt yourself becoming ineffective and unproductive? Have you ever attributed it to the fact that you are failing to persevere?

_____

What does Peter call those who are not persevering? (verse 9)

_____

_____

What have you lost sight of?

_____

That means when you have an argument or a bad day with your family, you are not defeated, regardless of the mistakes you made. You are forgiven, and because you are forgiven, you can start the next day with a new attitude and a repentant heart. Christ bought you at a price. That in itself is a reason to persevere. Christ's death not only forgave our sins, but our children's, our husband's, neighbor's, or anyone else we find ourselves in conflict with. Doesn't that change your perspective on the conflict? You are arguing with someone Christ laid down His life to forgive. If Christ laid down His life to forgive this person, how can you not forgive them, too?

Prayer to close the lesson:

Dear Father, I have fallen so short of being the salt and light of the world You intended me to be. Forgive me for not seeking Your will and Your ways more often in my daily life. Give me the strength to persevere with the situations in my life right now, and to wait patiently, with confidence, for Your deliverance. Let me never forget Your compassion or lose sight of Your mercy. In Jesus' name. Amen.

LESSON NINE: THE SIDONIAN WIDOW AND THE SHUNAMMITE WOMAN

Topics for Further Study: Hospitality, Tithing, and Our Bodies as Living Sacrifices

READ 1 KINGS 17:7–24; 2 KINGS 4:8–37.

Devotion: It is interesting to compare these two accounts that have so many similarities and some interesting differences, too. The woman at Sidon was widowed and living with her son in desperate poverty. She was down to her last meal with no hope to get more food. Helping Elijah was not an option for her, because she didn't have anything to offer him. Despite this, we're told in 1 Kings 17:9 that God commanded a widow to supply Elijah with food. We aren't told how the Lord commanded her to feed Elijah; just that God commanded her to give something she didn't have. To relate, think of something you don't have, say $50,000. Imagine God commanding you to give that to your church. For a busy mom, imagine God commanding you to take on a leadership role at your church, demanding one more thing of your time, which you don't have enough of as it is. The Shunammite woman was in completely different circumstances. She was well-to-do, living with her husband. In her wealth, she was generous to the Lord by providing meals and a place for Elisha to stay.

There are important Biblical truths to learn from these accounts. First, the Lord blesses obedience, especially when it requires faith. Later in the Shunnamite woman's life, Elisha told her to leave her house and go to another land in order to escape the famine that God was about to send for seven years on the land. She obeyed and when she returned seven years later, she went to the king to ask for her land back. Not only did he give her the land, but all the income that had been earned from the land during those seven years (2 Kings 8). It would not have been easy to leave her house and her country, but she obeyed and was rewarded for her obedience. The same was true for the Sidonian widow. She obeyed Elijah and made him some bread first, then found there was flour and oil enough for her and her son, not just that day, but every day after as well.

Second, the Lord will supply all our needs, even in desperate circumstances. When we study tithing in greater depth, we will see that God said when we give to him He will pour out his blessing on us. Jesus, too, assured us our heavenly Father knows our needs and will provide for us (Matthew 6:32).

The third principle is that how we treat others is the way we will be treated. In Luke 6:37 and 38, we are told, "Do not judge, and you will not be judged. Do not condemn and you will not be condemned. Forgive and you will be forgiven. Give and it will be given to you. A good measure, pressed down, shaken together and running over, will be poured into your lap. For with the measure you use, it will be measured to you."

Solomon gives further testimony to the same principle in Proverbs 11: "He who refreshes others will himself be refreshed" (11:25), and, "He who seeks good finds goodwill, but evil comes to him who searches for it" (11:27).

The widow at Sidon took care of Elijah, even if it was commanded of her, and God took care of her and her son, even raising the son from the dead.

In both accounts, we see the prophets staying in the homes of these women. The Sidonian widow offered hospitality reluctantly, but the Shunammite woman's hospitality was both willful and generous. The widow had a son already, whereas the Shunammite woman received a child in response to her generosity to the Lord.

When the boys became ill we see an extraordinary difference. Despite witnessing the daily miracle of God's provision, the widow watched her son die, and then accused Elijah of causing it. From her statement in 1 Kings 17:24 after Elijah raised her son, it's apparent she doubted Elijah's role as a prophet all along.

The Shunammite woman never doubted Elisha was "a holy man of God" (2 Kings 4:9). When her child died, she sought Elisha, and in seeking him, she sought the help of the Lord. Her faith was apparent as she assured her husband and Elisha's servant that everything was fine. She didn't worry and bother her husband, and she didn't wail and weep to the servant. She took all her emotions, her trust, and her faith and she fell at Elisha's feet. She knew her son's only hope was to be found at the feet of the Lord, and with unswerving faith she went there. What an example to us! So often in the depths of despair we waste precious time telling our woes to anyone who will listen, and we stress out our husbands and other family members instead of going to God, the only one able to help us.

The Shunnamite's response to Elisha bringing her son to life was to fall at Elisha's feet and bow to the ground. Doing so cannot be construed as an act of worship toward Elisha, but rather complete and total submission to the Lord. All along she has acknowledged God's existence and Elisha's role as a servant of God. Observing God's mercy and miraculous power firsthand, she couldn't help but fall once again before the Lord, this time out of gratitude.

These Biblical accounts show us that God uses all types of people to accomplish His will. He uses the rich and the poor, the willing heart and the reluctant, the person with a strong faith and the person struggling to believe. He bestowed the same miracle on both women, regardless of the attitude of the heart.

Sometimes God calls us to work with difficult people. You would think there would have been an agreeable widow in Elijah's own country who Elijah could have stayed with, but Jesus assures us Elijah was sent to the Sidonian widow because she was reluctant, but willing nonetheless, to help Elijah. "I tell you the truth,' [Jesus] continued, 'no prophet is accepted in his hometown. I assure you that there were many widows in Israel in Elijah's time, when the sky was shut for three and a half years and there was a severe famine in the land. Yet Elijah was not sent to any of them, but to a widow in Zarephath in the region of Sidon'" (Luke 4:24–26).

We often acquire the attitude of those we spend the most time with, just as Elijah blamed God for the child's death after the widow blamed him. That is why it is so important to return to God's Word at the end of the day and let Him have the last word. Often things become too much for us, and situations all around us look hopeless and out of control. We need to go back to the Lord so we remember that our God is the God who parted the Red Sea, brought life to barren women, destroyed Israel's enemies and rescued the Jews from sure annihilation (in the book of Esther).

He's also the God who's concerned about us and who knows the right time and the right way to work out the situations in our life. May we increasingly be like the Shunammite woman, being generous to the Lord, acknowledging the Lord, and fully trusting God's ability to do the impossible.

Devotion Question: Who is the holy man or woman of God in your life who you can go to for godly advice and prayer? What characteristics do they have that you would like to emulate?

Topics for Further Study:

1. Hospitality

   What is your idea of hospitality?

   _____

   _____

What are some ways you can show it?

_____

_____

Read 1 Peter 4:7–11.

Why should we practice hospitality? (verses 8,10)

_____

_____

What should our attitude be when we offer hospitality? (verse 9)

_____

_____

What does Peter say to the person who says it's too much work to invite people over or make meals for people in need? (verse 11)

_____

Who is glorified through your service?

_____

Read 3 John 5–8.

To whom should we offer hospitality?

_____

Why?

_____

_____

Read Hebrews 13:1, 2

What reason are we given for being hospitable?

_____

_____

2. **Tithing**

What is a tithe?

_____

Read Leviticus 27:30.

What was the commandment given through Moses to the Israelites regarding tithes?

_____

_____

Read Deuteronomy 14:22, 28, 29 and Malachi 3:8–12.

What will the Lord give us in exchange for our offerings?

_____

Read Genesis 4:2–8.

When did Cain bring his offering? (verse 3)

_____

When did Abel bring his offering? (verse 4)

_____

What kind of fruit did Cain bring and what kind of animals did Abel bring?

_____

_____

Why did God look with favor on Abel but not on Cain?

_____

_____

Cain offered "some" of his fruit "in the course of time" ... in other words, when he got around to it. Abel brought the best of his flock right from the beginning; the firstborn. Abel's gift shows a heart that loves the Lord and wants to honor God, whereas Cain was going through the motions.

What advice did God give Cain and to us regarding our gifts to Him? (verse 7)

_____

What advice did God give in regards to sin?

_____

Did Cain follow God's advice and master his sin?

_____

What does that tell you about letting sins go, or considering something "just a little sin"?

_____

Read Matthew 5:23-24; Luke 11:42.

What is God looking at when we offer a gift to Him?

_____

_____

_____

Why should we settle our disputes before giving our gifts to the Lord?

_____

God is concerned with our hearts and the attitude with which we give our offerings. If we are quarreling with our neighbor, our spouse, or our siblings, we are being obstinate and rebellious. When we seek peace in our relationships we are showing humility, love, and contrition. God delights in hearts that seek justice, love mercy and walk humbly with the Lord (Micah 6:8).

Read 2 Corinthians 9:6–11.

What does verse six mean?

_____

What is your attitude to be when you give to the Lord? (verse 7)

_____

_____

What blessing do you receive as a result of giving? (verses 10-11)

_____

What riches does God give His people?

_____

_____

Read Proverbs 11:24, 25.

What would you say to the person who says they just have no money to give to the Lord?

_____

_____

Read 1 Timothy 6:17–19.

What does Paul say to the wealthy?

_____

_____

3. Our Bodies as Living Sacrifices

Read Romans 12:1–8.

In what ways did the Shunnamite woman offer herself as a living sacrifice?

_____

What does Paul say we are doing when we live to serve God? (verse 1)

_____

_____

How do we do that? (verse 2)

_____

_____

Paul says we must set ourselves apart from the world and be transformed and have our minds renewed. The "world" is the media, the women in our lives who don't read their Bibles, and therefore do not know God's will, the entertainment industry, and every other thing that we are exposed to that either doesn't know God's will or rejects God's will and lives contrary to the principles God establishes in His Word. The "world" and the patterns of it will creep into our minds and hearts and souls every time we turn on the TV, go to a movie, and pick up a secular magazine. If you are allowing that into your head, you likely are conforming to the patterns you are seeing. Paul says, Stop! Set yourself apart from the world, turn off your TV, get rid of the gossip magazines, and get into God's Word so you understand God's ways. Then you can live in such a way as to please the Lord, and your way of life will be a means of worship.

What does "sober judgment" have to do with being a living sacrifice?

_____

_____

What must we have in order to use "sober judgment"? (verse 3)

_____

Without humility, we just may think we are gifted enough to do just about anything. We may even think we are more qualified than our pastors or other leaders in the church to get things done. There may be cases when that is true, but sober judgment is required to show it. Sober judgment and the humility that it requires allows us to recognize exactly which part of the body we are, so we can do our part, without crossing over to another member's job, and without seeking to accomplish our own goals, but rather carrying out God's will and going in the direction He leads us.

Make a list of your gifts.

_____

How are you using those gifts to serve the Lord?

_____

Read 1 Samuel 15:22; Psalm 40:6–8; Psalm 51:17; Proverbs 21:3; and Hosea 6:6.

All these passages point to the condition of our heart. To fast and keep the Sabbath a day of rest are good things, but if our heart is not poised to obey and our hands and feet and mouth do not desire to serve the Lord, any and all sacrifice is in vain. If we give twenty percent of our income to the church, but turn our backs on our neighbor who needs help, or complain when our mother-in-law needs help, we have missed the point entirely. God wants hearts that are in tune to Him. That's how Jesus lived. He had compassion on the crowds, on the sick, and on the sinners. He lived to show mercy. He healed on the Sabbath, and His disciples did not fast, because he was concerned most with the condition of a person's heart.

What is the condition of your heart?

_____

Are you seeking to accomplish your goals or God's?

_____

Prayer to close the lesson:

I come before You, holy and merciful Father, repentant for failing to serve You the way I should. Forgive me for so often being like the Sidonian widow, reluctant to help, and helping with a poor or cynical attitude. Pour Your Spirit into my heart that I may be more like You. Remind me often that, "The earth is the Lord's and everything in it." Hospitality and tithing are so much easier when I remember all that I have is Yours. In the name of my Lord and Savior I pray. Amen.

Lesson Ten: Elizabeth

Topics for Further Study: The Omniscience of God, How to Respond to God's Call in Our Lives, and Glorifying God Through Obedience.

Read Luke 1:5–25, 39–45, 57–66.

Devotion: God chose an upright, childless couple that had been praying for a child to be the parents of John the Baptist. Unlike Samson's father, Manoah, who believed the promise of a son before even seeing the angel of the Lord, Zechariah doubted even when the angel appeared to him. Different people have different gifts. Some have a faith that won't waiver. Others encourage. Still others pray. Just because Zechariah was a priest didn't mean he was immune to having a faith that didn't falter.

This brings us to an important point regarding our children. Though born of the same womb, each of them has been specially designed for a purpose God intended. God blesses each in different ways, which is how one can be such a help with chores, while the other is easily distracted. One may be studious, while the other struggles. One is athletic, another musical. Surely God has a purpose in mind for all of our children, and we need only to trust Him, while building our children up in their strengths and helping them in the areas where they struggle.

Gabriel's answer to Zechariah is one to be noted. "I am Gabriel. I stand in the presence of God and have been sent to speak to you and to tell you this good news" (Luke 1:19). When Jesus walked on the earth, He was a humble man, but as Gabriel reminds us, we should never forget the omniscience and omnipotence of God. This is the God, after all, who parted not just the Jordan River, but the Red Sea, who brought His prophet home to heaven in a flaming chariot, who brought life from barren wombs! Jesus performed so many miracles, the apostle John said that, if written down, the whole world would not be able to contain the books (John 21:25). Gabriel's statement serves as a reminder to give God the respect He deserves in our thoughts, our prayers, and in His house.

Elizabeth, though she is old, does not have such a hard time accepting the miraculous gift. She gives glory to God, getting past the hardship she endured for so many years to enjoy the blessing God saved for her for that time.

When Mary came to visit Elizabeth, we see Elizabeth acting as a vessel of the Holy Spirit. Despite Elizabeth's age, she humbled herself before Mary, acknowledging the supremacy of Christ. This is a foreshadowing of when John and Jesus met and John responded likewise: "I need to be baptized by you, and do you come to me?" (Matthew 3:14). Elizabeth and John approached their roles in God's kingdom with humble servitude. Elizabeth is a perfect example of what Paul describes later in Romans 12 and 1 Corinthians 12. In Christ we are all one body, though we each have a different role. Unlike the people of Corinth, Elizabeth and later John were able to accept "the weaker and less honorable role" (1Corinthians 12:22-23) with grace. By doing so, they left room for God to raise them up. Jesus said, "Whoever wants to be great among you must be your servant, and whoever wants to be first must be a slave to all. For even the Son of Man did not come to be served, but to serve, and to give his life as a ransom for many" (Mark 10:43–45).

Another point of significance about Elizabeth's greeting was the way it was done. Luke said, "In a loud voice she exclaimed" her praises (Luke 1:42). God had done great things for and around Elizabeth, and Elizabeth was not shy about letting it be known. So often the voice of dissent is much louder than that of praise. Look, too, how the praise given by Elizabeth spurs Mary to give praise as well. Attitudes are contagious. We should work hard to have one that encourages others and glorifies God for the great things He has done for and around us.

Finally, we see Elizabeth glorifying God in obedience when it came to John's name. The angel gave Zechariah John's name, and with Elizabeth we see, despite the protest from relatives, she persevered in reverence and submission to God's will.

It is not always easy to do what God shows us we should do. Often those closest to us are the ones who disapprove. Elizabeth shows us that when the Lord points us in a direction, we would do well to follow, despite opposition from friends or family.

If Zechariah and Elizabeth were alive as John grew, it could not have been easy for them to watch what unfolded before them. John lived a desolate life in the desert. This was necessary to fulfill the prophecy that referred to him as, "A voice of one" (Isaiah 40:3). It also, no doubt, served as a vehicle for fellowship with God, the isolation serving as a quiet medium for prayer, and a heart and mind receptive to God's will.[14] He did not concern himself with the problems of city or family life. He suffered ridicule, imprisonment, and finally, death by beheading. Yet, Jesus said about him, "I tell you the truth: Among those born of women there has not risen anyone greater than John the Baptist" (Matthew 11:11).

In moments of hardship with our children, when we watch things happen to them that are not fair, it would be good for us to remember what happens on earth is for a moment, a day or two, or maybe a few years. Eternity is what we wait for, what we look forward to, and what we need to focus on with our children, that we may spend it together.

Devotion Question: Have you discovered your role in life? For most of Elizabeth's life she was not a mother. Her actions in the accounts we read show her to be an encourager, and a facilitator of God's will. How will you be remembered? How sad if people were to remember you for always complaining or for the wrench you threw in people's plans. It is never too late to change. Consider how others think of you and write down what traits family, friends, and co-workers might use to describe you. Determine to change your negative attributes.

Topics for Further Study:

1. The Omniscience of God

Read Job 38:1–21; 41:10,11; 42:1–6, and Isaiah 40:12–28.

What characteristics of God are revealed to us in these passages?

_____

_____

My husband works on old cars and when he gets around another man who knows about cars, the two of them can name things I will never know or understand. That's how I feel when reading the above readings. God knows His creation like the back of His hand. He knows the oceans, the mountains, the stars, the animals, the attributes of each and how they work together.

If we were to read the rest of Job chapters 38, 39, and 40, we would hear of God's gifts to different animals. He assures us that He intentionally created each with certain attributes. What significance is that to us?

_____

Read Jeremiah 33:3 and Romans 11:33.

What does the word "unsearchable" mean in these passages?

_____

Read Ecclesiastes 11:5; Isaiah 55:8, 9 and Daniel 8:15, 16, and 27.

How much about God do we understand?

_____

_____

Why is that?

_____

_____

_____

2. **How are we to respond to God's call in our lives?**

Read Isaiah 6:1–8.

Compare and contrast Isaiah's calling with Zechariah's experience with Gabriel.

_____

_____

Read Matthew 4:18–22; Matthew 9:9, and Mark 10:17–22.

What can we learn from the calling of these men?

_____

_____

Read Matthew 9:35–38 and Romans 12:1–8.

How do we know when God is calling us to do something?

_____

_____

What, if anything, is hindering you from answering God's call in your life? For Zechariah, it was the need to be reassured of God's desire. For the rich young man, it was his things. Is your house, job, hobbies, or anything else keeping you from answering God's call to serve?

_____

_____

Read Revelation 2:8–10 and 7:9–17.

Will service to God be easy?

_____

Why is it worth our while to follow those calls? After all, the disciples died cruel deaths, and people tried to kill Isaiah and ridiculed him mercilessly.

_____

Does God call us to do different things today than He did in Jeremiah's time? What does God call us to do today? Think about that question in terms of your family, your community, and finally, the world.

3. Glorifying God through obedience

Read John 12:27,28 and John 17:4.

These passages talk about Jesus' purpose on earth. What is our purpose on earth?

_____

_____

Read Jeremiah 1:4–12 and 17–19.

What does this account teach us about responding to God in obedience?

_____

How do you feel when you ask your children to do something when you have guests in your house if they obey you without grumbling or hesitation?

_____

How do you feel when they refuse to obey in front of other people, or do so with whining and complaining?

_____

_____

Make a list of things the world permits and encourages, but which God instructs us not to do. I'll use drinking as an example. Ephesians 5:18 says, "Do not get drunk on wine, which leads to debauchery. Instead, be filled with the Spirit." When a person professing to be a Christian goes out with the full knowledge and intent of drinking too much, that person is acting in disobedience to God, and rebelling against God's law. By thumbing a nose at God, that person tells everyone else, by their example, it is not important to obey God. They have completely muted any chance they may have had at winning someone to Christ. Why would someone else obey God's commands if you aren't? What other things does the world permit or encourage that God forbids?

_____

_____

Read Hebrews 10:26–29 and 1 John 3:4–10.

According to Hebrews 10:29, what two things are we doing when we deliberately sin?

_____

_____

When you choose to not know God's commands, because you choose not to spend time in God's Word, is your sinning deliberate?

_____

The people of Martin Luther's day did not have access to the Bible, but we have access not just to the written Word, but also to CDs and DVDs that allow us to listen or watch the Word. What excuse can you give God as to why you can't spend time in His Word?

_____

Since we all sin and fall short of the glory of God (Romans 3:23), how can we live up to what John says in 3:7–9?

_____

Remember, God looks on the heart. He sees your motives and your intentions and He rewards effort. Spending time in God's Word on a daily basis will keep both the law and gospel in front of you. With that, we will be reminded of what God sees as sin and how He has called us to live, and we will also be reminded of His grace when we fall short. To not be in God's Word and to be going off our own ideas as to what we perceive to be good or bad is disastrous. The devil is the master of deception and works to convince us all kinds of sins are not bad, or as bad as others. Obeying God's commands is glorifying to God, but it is also a means of distinguishing yourself as a true child of God.

Jesus said many will say, "'Sir, open the door for us.' But he will answer, 'I don't know you or where you come from.' Then you will say, 'We ate and drank with you, and you taught in our streets.' But he will reply, 'I don't know you or where you come from. Away from me, all you evildoers!'" (Luke 13:25–27).

Did you notice the people calling to Him ate and drank with Him and heard Him teach? These are people in the church. It is not enough to go to church and then live however you please. The writer of Hebrews says the person who does that tramples on Christ's crucifixion and insults the Holy Spirit. Pray that God would work in you that you may glorify Him through obedience. To begin, spend time in the Word every day, so you can know God and His commands.

Prayer to close the lesson:

Heavenly Father, how can I approach You, except in humble submission? I am a mere infant in my thoughts and actions, yet so often I think I know how to run my life and others'. Forgive me for the many times You've watched me make a mess of things, and more, forgive me for trampling on Christ's crucifixion with my sin. Let me learn Your ways so my life glorifies You. When You come to me, help me to respond as Your chosen ones, saying, "Here I am. Send me." When my days are over, bring me to You and to the place where all Your saints rest. In Christ I pray. Amen.

LESSON 11: MARY

Topics for Further Study: Humility vs. Pride, Giving Glory to God, and The Importance of Christian Fellowship

READ LUKE 1:26–38.

Devotion: The angel of the Lord announced the births of Isaac, Samson, John the Baptist, and now Jesus. Sarah laughed, Samson's parents asked for direction, Zechariah asked for a sign. Only Mary responded with humble submission.

The obvious difference is the other couples had been trying unsuccessfully for years to have children. Perhaps for Mary, above all the others, this came as an interruption in her own plans to get married soon and start a life with Joseph, which made her complete acceptance of it even more commendable.

It is interesting that Mary didn't worry about what her parents or Joseph or anyone else would think when the angel told her she would have a baby. In Jewish society at that time, Mary ran the risk of being stoned to death. Her pregnancy out of wedlock was a violation of her promise to Joseph. Mary might have asked the angel to explain the situation to her parents or fiancé, and indeed the angel did explain it in a dream to Joseph, but not because Mary asked, unless she asked later privately in prayer.

What we see in Mary is unswerving faith that if God wanted this to happen, He would make the necessary arrangements for it to work out. Mary said to the angel and to God, "I am the Lord's servant…. May it be to me as you have said" (Luke 1:38). Scripture provides further evidence of this when Elizabeth, at the Holy Spirit's prompting, says, "Blessed is she who has believed that what the Lord has said to her will be accomplished!" (Luke 1:45).

How often doesn't God move us in a certain direction in our lives, but we push His plans aside for a more convenient time, or at least until we can arrange all the details? We plan to see that ailing friend just as soon as we aren't so busy at work, or promise to teach the girl's group at church how to sew, but not until after basketball season. We say we'll find time to read our Bible when our life isn't so hectic.

Mary teaches us the proper way to respond to God's prompting. "Yes, Lord, I am your servant. What would you like me to do?" Her trust in God shows Mary's respect for His supremacy. How often we rely on a human who is subject to errors in judgment and faulty reasoning, but question when the Lord prompts us to do His will. Instead of trying to work God's plans into our lives, how much better to do what God asks and pray for the strength to do the rest of our work as well. This is what Jesus was talking about when He said, "Seek first his kingdom and his righteousness, and all these things will be given to you as well" (Matthew 6:33).

That is what Mary did. She put God and His plan for her life above everything, even Joseph's considerations. Carrying a baby and the Son of God certainly had implications for Joseph, but Mary remembered that even before she was a fiancée to Joseph, she was God's servant. Certainly it is OK to make plans, but the pinnacle of servitude is really reached when we can say to the Lord, "Here I am. Show me what you want me to do today."

James puts this into further perspective. "Now listen, you who say, 'Today or tomorrow we will go to this or that city, spend a year there, carry on business and make money.' Why, you do not even know what will happen tomorrow. What is your life? You are a mist that appears for a little while and then vanishes. Instead, you ought to say, 'If it is the Lord's will, we will live and do this or that'" (James 4:13–15).

It is also important for us to remember that when things aren't quite going the way we hoped, often that's God's way of saying we're trying to do something He hadn't planned for us, or we're doing or seeking something that would cause more harm than good in our lives. Proverbs 19:21 says, "Many are the plans in a man's heart, but it is the Lord's purpose that prevails."

When we are walking with the Lord, He puts us where He needs us at each phase of our lives. Sometimes that is in the guise of a different job, or home, or another child. If we aren't putting the Lord first, or second, or in our top priorities at all, and if we aren't praying for wisdom and direction, we can certainly find ourselves in a job that requires more of our time than we had hoped, or in a home that demands a lot of our money, or making decisions about the number of children we should have flippantly or based on our own selfishness. We certainly are capable of making bad decisions if we are blindly walking through life.

In Genesis 13, Abraham let Lot choose the land he wanted when their shepherds could no longer get along and their flocks were too great for the land to support them both. Though Abraham was older than Lot, he submitted to Lot's decision, and Lot chose the best of the land, leaving second best for Abraham. Not long afterward, an army carried Lot away and Abraham rescued him (Genesis 14). Not long after that, God destroyed Sodom and Gomorrah and Lot barely escaped with his life, losing his wife in the process (Genesis 19). God blessed Abraham, even though Abraham did not determine where his flocks or his house would be.

So often we feel we have to control everything in our lives, but these accounts show us God can and will bless us even when we are put into a situation by no effort or decision on our part. In fact, it is often because we don't quit serving the Lord despite where we've been put that the Lord blesses us.

It was not because of a fault on Joseph's part that he was sold into slavery, but because of his brothers' jealousy. Look how the Lord blessed him. He became second in command in all of Egypt (Genesis 37 and 41). Rahab didn't ask for the spies to come to her house, they just showed up. Just as likely as not, she wished she didn't have to deal with them at that time. Despite this, she did what was right by God, and because of it, her family was spared. She certainly could have died if the king found out she was lying. Mary, Abraham, Joseph, and Rahab all show us to trust God when we are displaced, and when life changes in an instant and our circumstances are never the same. Blessings will follow if we continue to trust.

Another important aspect of this account is that when the miracle of Elizabeth's pregnancy is revealed to Mary, that's who she goes to. Doing so does not disappoint her. Elizabeth affirmed everything the angel revealed to Mary. That is one benefit of Christian fellowship. Men, and especially for us mothers, other women who remind us of God's faithfulness, are an invaluable resource. A friend who is willing to pray with us during our darkest moments or share scripture verses proves to be a member of God's army to shield us and protect us from temptation. An encouragement at just the right time is often exactly what we need to keep the faith when Satan is trying to pull us away.

Mary's life came to a complete halt with the angel's message. For 33 years she would be watching things she didn't fully understand, but the Lord kept other Christians around her to strengthen her. He offered Elizabeth at first, then shepherds and wisemen to reaffirm that Jesus was no ordinary child, but the long-awaited Savior. Later, when Jesus was too busy to see her, she had her other children, and the other women who followed Jesus caring for His needs. At the cross, Jesus provided John, the disciple closest to him, to watch over her and take care of her.

God has promised to never leave or forsake us. At the point

when we don't know if we can go on, He always offers help, whether in the form of family members, friends, a sermon that says exactly what we need to hear, or something else.

Like Mary, we need only to go through life saying to the Lord, whatever comes our way, "I am your servant. May it be to me, whatever you want, because I trust You to see me through whatever you give me." What peace we have when we leave our lives totally in God's hands.

Devotion Question: Have you considered the interruptions in your life to be speed bumps from God telling you to slow down and look to Him for guidance before proceeding? What interruptions have occurred in your life lately? What is God telling you? If you don't know, start praying for insight.

Topics for Further Study:

1. **Humility vs. Pride**

   Read Philippians 2:3.

   What is humility?

   _____

   Read Titus 3:1–5.

   Why are we to be humble?

   _____

Read 2 Chronicles 7:14 and Zephaniah 1:18–2:3.

Of what benefit is it to us to humble ourselves before the Lord?

_____

What, besides humility, does the Lord ask of us in these passages?

_____

Read Proverbs 16:5; Proverbs18:12, and James 4:6.

How does the Lord feel about pride?

_____

What will happen to the proud?

_____

Read Isaiah 2:11.

What do we fail to do when we act in pride?

_____

Read James 4:6–10, 16.

What does God do for us when we seek Him with humility? (verses 6, 10)

_____

_____

How do we go about humbling ourselves before the Lord? (verses 8, 9)

_____

_____

2. **Giving Glory to God**

Read 2 Kings 5:1–16.

Who did Naaman credit with his healing? (verse 15)

_____

Who did the Israelite girl say could heal Naaman? (verse 3)

_____

Who did Elisha say would cure Naaman? (verse 8)

_____

Why didn't Naaman credit Elisha?

_____

What was Elisha's role? (verses 8, 15)

_____

What was the difference between the king and Elisha?

_____

Though the slave girl told Naaman the prophet would cure Naaman, Naaman seemed to understand Elisha's role as an instrument used by God. A piano can not play itself anymore than Elisha could heal. Only God could heal and He chose Elisha as the one to deliver the instructions. The credit, however, belonged to God and God alone.

Read Ruth 1:3–5, 4:13–15.

Why didn't Ruth have any children with her first husband?

_____

How was she able to have a child with Boaz?

_____

Who did the women credit when Obed was born?

_____

Read Daniel 6:16–23.

_____

How did the king describe Daniel? (verses 16, 20)

_____

_____

Because of the way Daniel lived before this incident, the king knew it was only God who could save Daniel. As always, Daniel gave credit to God. How would people describe you? Do they know you have a God, and would they say about you, "Servant of the living God, whom you serve continually?"

How did Daniel's life give glory to God?

_____

_____

How does your lifestyle either glorify or debase God?

_____

Read 2 Corinthians 10:12–18.

What did Paul not want to do? (verses 12, 16)

_____

What does it mean to "boast in the Lord?"

_____

_____

What sort of approval ought we to seek? (verse 18)

_____

Read Galatians 6:14.

If we have a claim to fame, what should it be?

_____

3. The Importance of Christian Fellowship

Read Hebrews 10:24, 25.

Of what benefit is Christian fellowship to us?

_____

Read 1 Corinthians 16:15–18.

What did Stephanas, Fortunatus, and Achaicus do for Paul? (verses 17, 18)

_____

Read Romans 12:10–16.

Paul gives us some guidelines for Christian fellowship. What are they?

Be _____ to one another.

_____ one another.

Never be _____.

Be _____ in hope,

_____ in affliction,

_____ in prayer.

_____ with God's people in need.

Practice _____.

_____ those who persecute you.

_____ with those who

_____,

_____with those who

_____.

Live in _____.

Do not be _____ or

_____.

Which of these are you good at?

_____

Which do you need to work on?

_____

Read 1 Corinthians 1:9.

We are in fellowship with whom?

_____

Knowing you are sharing fellowship with Jesus, how does that make you want to act?

_____

Read Philippians 2:1, 2.

What do you need to have the truest sort of Christian fellowship? (verse 2)

_____

Prayer to close the lesson

Holy Father, help me to be willing to serve You when You call, without hesitation or selfish concerns. Provide for me all that I need to carry out the plans You set before me. Thank You for the blessing of Christian friends, to encourage, support and spur me on. May all I do bring glory to You. I pray in Jesus' name. Amen.

LESSON 12: SALOME

Topics for Further Study: Busyness, Heaven, and The Heart of a Servant

READ MATTHEW 20:20–24; 27: 55-56; MARK 16:1–8.

Devotion: By putting the gospel accounts of Matthew 27:56 and Mark 16:1 together, we can surmise that Salome was the mother of James and John, and the wife of Zebedee. When Jesus called James and John out of the boat with their father Zebedee, it appears they did an incredible thing. Once you read of their mother, you see their mother was a dedicated follower of Jesus, too. We aren't told if Jesus called James and John first, or if Salome had already started following Jesus. We can be certain following Jesus was a family affair.

James and John were two of the threesome often allowed into the inner circle with Jesus. Peter, James, and John witnessed the transfiguration (Mark 9:2), they were the only disciples to witness Jairus' daughter being raised from the dead (Mark 5:37), and they went with Jesus to pray in Gethsemane the night He was arrested (Mark 14:33).

Salome also witnessed amazing things. She was there with Mary, the mother of Jesus, watching Jesus die (Mark 15:40). She was there Easter morning at the empty tomb and saw and heard from the angel that Jesus was no longer dead. No doubt, throughout her travels with Jesus, she had seen and heard many other things.

The Bible portrays people as they were, showing both the good and bad. Because of that, we're given the account of Salome coming to Jesus and asking that her sons sit at His sides in glory. This isn't a request made in humility. Rather, it is taking our worldly idea of status and trying to apply it to heaven.

Sometimes, unfortunately, we see the same thing being done within the church. Anytime a person is seeking status, pride has entered his or her heart. Status seekers are those people who announce their good works. They are the ones trying to befriend the pastor and other church leaders just for the sake of being around leaders. Status seekers sing the praises of the pastor and church leaders, even when their actions are not Biblical. The problem with status seekers in the church is they are failing to impress God, who is the true head of the church. God is impressed with a person who does good works to help another person, but doesn't let anyone else know about it (Matthew 6:3). God is impressed with humility and someone who will stand up for Him and what is Biblical and right, even if it means a necessary confrontation that makes us uncomfortable.

Jesus showed Salome, and us, that to follow Him was to live contrary to the world. The world seeks wealth. God's people are to keep themselves free from the love of money and be content

(Hebrews 13:5). The world looks highly on rank and position. Jesus said greatness is found in service (Matthew 20:26, 27). The world says eat, drink, and be merry. God says we must give an account for all our actions (Matthew 12:36, Hebrews 4:13) and if we have lived to please ourselves only, neglecting those who need help, we are in jeopardy of becoming one of those to whom Jesus says, "I tell you the truth, I don't know you" (Matthew 25:12). The writer of the book of James sums it up this way: "Don't you know that friendship with the world is hatred toward God? Anyone who chooses to be a friend of the world becomes an enemy of God" (James 4:4).

Despite her momentary lapse in judgment, Salome had a significant role in Jesus' ministry, caring for Jesus' physical needs. What an awesome privilege she had. We know her husband had a fishing business, and Salome had two sons and no doubt a house or a place where her family lived. But Jesus was a priority to her. Even with all the other busyness around her, she chose to serve her Lord.

We have that same choice to make today. While Jesus is not walking the earth physically today, the needs of the invisible church at large are great. Not everyone can go on a missionary trip to Africa, but most families could give regularly to a ministry that helps missions. Not everyone can teach Sunday school, but perhaps you could design projects to go with each lesson if that is your gift. If you can cook or bake, offer to bring food for a funeral, and if you have the time, serve food for that grieving family.

Serving Jesus is not only done at church. Serving our Lord is done when we shovel our elderly neighbor's walk for them, or take food to a person who has been sick. Serving the Lord can be as easy as sending an encouraging card, or praying for someone who is struggling. Jesus said, "Anyone who gives you a cup of water in my name because you belong to Christ will certainly not lose his reward" (Mark 9:41). In fact, Jesus says, "I tell you the truth, whatever you did for one of the least of these brothers of mine, you did for me" (Matthew 25:40). In other words, anytime we see someone in need of something and we help him or her, it is as if we are helping Jesus. Salome, we are told, "had followed Jesus from Galilee to care for his needs" (Matthew 27:55), and we will be like her if we live our lives being tuned into people's needs. Even more than being like her, we will be like Jesus, who set the example for her. It is important to do these things, not just for people in our church, but also for those outside the body of Christ, so they have a chance to experience the love of Christ flowing through us. The goal is to become proactive so information isn't lost on you. Become one of those who "[does] not withhold good from those who deserve it, when it is in your power to act" (Proverbs 3:27).

When Salome bowed down before Jesus and asked Him to give her sons thrones next to Christ, she didn't have the heart of a servant. No doubt by the time Jesus died, she did. How could she not after her years following Jesus, the ultimate servant? May we, too, strive to be like Salome and follow Jesus and make his teachings and actions our own.

Devotion Question: In James 2, James talks about treating the poor man and rich man at church alike; not being a status seeker. We could say treat the young man with piercings and tattoos the same as the mother of three, or the distinguished old man. When is the last time you sought a person out at church to talk to, whether young or old, who might not feel comfortable? Are you going out of your way to make people feel at home in God's house? Are you willing to go beyond your circle of friends at church to seek out someone else? How about in your neighborhood and at work?

Topics for Further Study:

1. Busyness

Read Isaiah 32:6.

What is the foolish man failing to recognize?

_____

Why can't he see other people's needs?

_____

Are you too busy to notice or care about the needs of those around you?

_____

Read Haggai 1:9–11.

Why did the Lord refuse to send rain upon the land?

_____

What were the people preoccupied with?

_____

Has your house become a preoccupation to you?

Read Luke 9:59–62.

The note in my NIV study Bible points out that the man didn't have a dead father to bury. If his father had died he would already be busy with preparations. The man was saying, let me live with my father until he dies; after that, I will follow you.

Who got in the way of these two men following Jesus? What were they putting first?

_____

You may be saying, wait a minute. That man wanted to stay with his aging father. And to not let that man say good-bye to his family seems harsh. In fact, I can hear someone saying, if Jesus expects me to turn my back on my family then count me out!

It's ironic how when we turn our backs on our family and their needs we expect the Lord to understand. When our husband comes to bed wanting some attention and we're tired and shoo him away we tell ourselves God doesn't really expect us to please our husband after the full day we put in at work or home and the hours we spent getting the kids fed and bathed afterwards, right?

Titus 2:4-5 says, "Train the younger women to love their husbands and children…. and to be subject to their husbands so that no one will malign the word of God."

When our children cry out in the middle of the night and we get up and treat them harshly, we can so easily excuse our actions, but we expect the Lord to answer us if we cry out to Him anytime, day or night.

When your mother-in-law calls to let you know her apple tree split in half and is sprawled across the yard and you say to your husband, "You've got more than enough to do here. She can hire someone to take care of that" and encourage him to not help his mother, we feel justified. But in some cases, following Jesus would mean putting aside the things you need to get done at home, and helping your mother-in-law. My mother-in-law, for instance, is a widow. Paul tells Timothy, "Give proper recognition to those widows who are really in need. But if a widow has children or grandchildren, these should learn first of all to put their religion into practice by caring for their own family and so repaying their parents and grandparents, for this is pleasing to God" (1 Timothy 5:3,4).

Jesus is reminding us that we can always find ways to keep busy with our families and in doing so, excuse ourselves from doing God's work. We all have houses to clean and laundry to do and food to make. As someone who often is looking for volunteers for different events at church, I can assure you it is a wonderful thing to have someone answer without hesitation that they can help.

That is what Jesus is talking about. The person who is eager and ready to help digs in and gets to work. They look ahead to getting the job done. Jesus said those people who start a job, then begin looking at things they could be doing elsewhere, are not fit for service in the kingdom of God. Their minds and their hearts are on earthly things.

Certainly we all have different seasons of life and the Lord does not expect us to miss our son's basketball game in order to set up chairs at church for a seminar. If, however, you are going for coffee and donuts, or to do some child-free grocery shopping while your children are in Sunday school, perhaps you could be offering your services. If you don't have time for service in God's kingdom, but you have an evening line-up of your favorite TV shows, God is not a priority to you.

Read 2 Thessalonians 3:11–13 and Titus 2:4, 5.

Paul tells us to keep busy in these passages. Why?

_____

On the one hand we are told to keep busy and on the other hand to keep from being so involved in our own lives that we don't have time to help anyone. Helping other people can keep you very busy. Paul tells us being busy keeps us from sinning, but we need to make sure we are busy doing the right things. Being on different sports teams can be a good way to get exercise and keep up friendships, but if it takes time away from our family and revolves around the drinking that happens after the game, it's not the best use of our time. Sometimes we are "busy" because we are irresponsible with our time, or making earthly things a priority. Each of us is given only so much time on this earth. How are you spending your days? Are you living to satisfy your own pleasures? Would God be pleased with the way you are spending your time? If not, what can you do differently?

_____

Read Luke 5:15,16; 6:12; 9:18; 11:1.

Despite the crowds that needed to be taught, comforted, and healed, what did Jesus take time to do?

_____

In your busyness has your prayer life flourished, or suffered, or is it non-existent?

_____

Prayer is your communication line to God. If you aren't praying you aren't talking to God, and all relationships suffer if you don't spend time talking. Make prayer a priority. Spend at least as much time praying as you spend talking to your mother, or the person you are closest to.

2. Heaven

Read Deuteronomy 26:15 and 1 Kings 22:19.

What is heaven?

_____

Read Matthew 5:12; Luke 12:32-34; and 1 Peter 1:3,4.

What will we have in heaven?

_____

Read Luke 16:20, 25; and Philippians 3:20–21.

What will be different about our bodies?

_____

Read Revelation 20:11–15.

We should not misunderstand John's vision of the judgment to think we are saved "according to what we have done," meaning somehow our good works are a means of gaining access into heaven. In the book of James, we read, "As the body without the spirit is dead, so faith without deeds is dead" (James 2:26). Jesus said, "I am the true vine, and my Father is the gardener. He cuts off every branch in me that bears no fruit, while every branch that does bear fruit he prunes so that it will be even more fruitful" (John 15:1, 2). Our works are a reflection of what is in our heart, and if we are alive in Christ our works will naturally reflect that.

The sea giving up those who died in it is reminiscent of the army of Israel being brought back to life from the pile of bones in Ezekiel chapter thirty-seven. No matter what sort of death our loved ones have had, God is able to put their bodies back together, and some day He will do that.

How does this account of judgment make you feel?

_____

Are you sure of where you will end up when God's judgment on you is announced? What about your loved ones and friends and neighbors?

_____

It is easy to get wrapped up in our own lives and think our friends and relatives who don't know the Lord have a right to feel how they want, so we leave them alone. However, I'm not sure we will feel that way if we have to watch them being thrown into hell. If we try to talk to them about Jesus and are not successful, then pray for them, earnestly, but at least try, and don't give up on prayer.

Read Colossians 4:2–6.

What tangible things can you do to tell unbelievers in your life about the Lord?

_____

Paul breaks it down like this: be in prayer, make the most of every opportunity. When an unbeliever in your life falls into misfortune; losing a job or a loved one being in an accident, be the first to step in with a meal or to offer prayers. Let your words be encouraging and loving. Then they will know us by our love. That just may open a door to sharing the gospel.

_____

Read Revelation 21:3–8, 22; 22:6.

Who will not be in heaven?

_____

_____

What are some of the attributes of our heavenly home?

_____

Heaven is the Garden of Eden minus the chance to fall. The tree of knowledge of good and evil is gone, the curse is gone, and man will dwell with God again, this time for eternity. There are all kinds of things we don't know, and we aren't given answers to them. But, God gave us what we need to know; that heaven is our inheritance (Revelation 21:7) and we will not be in need, nor will we have pain, or cry, or mourn.

Read John 11:26 and Acts 16:30-31.

How do we get to heaven?

_____

After reading about the judgment and the lake of fire and the glory of heaven, what are your priorities? What do you want to teach your children?

_____

3. The Heart of a Servant

Read Matthew 26:39 and John 6:38.

Who was Jesus' master? Who set the agenda for Jesus' life?

_____

Read Mark 14:33–36.

Did Jesus struggle at times to do the will of the Father?

_____

Who sets the agenda for your life?

_____

Read Ephesians 6:5–8 and Colossians 3:23,24.

What incentive do we have to serve willingly, whether at home, at church, in our community, or at work? Who are we really serving?

_____

Look at the things you do around your house: making supper, cleaning the bathroom, taking care of the kids. Would you do things differently if you were doing them for Jesus instead of your husband or children? What about the things at church? Would you prepare differently if Jesus were coming instead of a group of ladies, or your Sunday school class?

_____

Read Luke 17:7–10.

What should your attitude be when you are serving the Lord?

_____

_____

Read Matthew 6:1–4.

Do you find yourself waiting for someone else to volunteer to do something or comparing how much you've done to how much others are doing? What does this passage teach us about service?

Prayer to close the lesson:

Holy Father, be Lord and Master of my life. Help me to remember in everything I do that following You is what matters most. Forgive me for the times when my pride and selfish ambition have robbed You of my time and energy. Forgive me for the wasted days and nights I've worried and/or dreamed of high positions here on earth. Give me the heart of a servant, and let my service glorify You. In Jesus' name I pray. Amen.

NOTES

1. Dr. Herbert Lockyer, R.S.L., All The Women of the Bible (Grand Rapids, Michigan: Zondervan Publishing House), 155.

2. Noah Webster, Webster's II New Riverside Dictionary (New York: Berkley Books, 1984), 692

3. Webster, "Webster's II New Riverside Dictionary," 220.

4. Robert Fitzgerald, Minnesota Independence Party Candidate for Senate, November 2006.

5. The ideas in this paragraph were influenced by Dr. James Dobson and his principles of discipline and love and the necessary balance of the two. For further study see Dr. Dobson's books "Dare to Discipline" and "The Strong-Willed Child."

6. Concordia Self-study Bible New International Version (St. Louis:Concordia Publishing House, 1986) 1515.

7. This section of passages was taken from: David P. Kuske, The Small Catechism of Dr. Martin Luther and an Exposition

for Children and Adults Written in Contemporary English (Milwaukee, Wisconsin, 1982), 80.

8. Kuske, "The Small Catechism of Dr. Martin Luther and an Exposition for Children and Adults," 83.

9. I recommend "Living Love" by Debbie Alsdorf published by Cook Communications, 2000.

10. I first heard about "wise words" on a radio Bible study on Abigail. That study aired on "Revive Our Hearts" by Nancy Lee DeMoss, September 5, 2005.

11. Concordia Self-study Bible New International Version, 455.

12. Webster, "Webster's II New Riverside Dictionary," 431.

13. Webster, "Webster's II New Riverside Dictionary," 664.

14. All the Women of the Bible, 51.

12571086R00111

Made in the USA
Monee, IL
26 September 2019